The NTCA Throws Handbook

Edited by

James A. Peterson, Ph.D., FACSM

and

Rob Lasorsa

ISBN: 978-1-58518-004-2
Library of Congress Control Number: 2006937667
Cover design: Bean Creek Studio
Book layout: Bean Creek Studio
Front cover photo: (L) Gary M. Prior/Getty Images Sport (R) Andy Lyons/Getty Images Sport
Back cover photo: Herb Fitzer

Coaches Choice
P.O. Box 1828
Monterey, CA 93942
www.coacheschoice.com

To the six individuals inducted in 2005 into the first-ever NTCA Throwers Hall of Fame class. By deed and example, you set a hallmark of excellence for every throws athlete and coach who has ever participated in our great sport.

Dedication

Acknowledgments

The National Throws Coaches Association is tremendously appreciative of the coaches who have contributed to this manual. We are extremely grateful for their support.

I would also like to thank the members of the NTCA Executive Committee: Mark Heckel, Gary Aldrich, Bruce Van Horne, Mark Harsha, Joe Napoli, Matt Ellis, Gerry McEvoy, and Glenn Thompson. The executive committee has voluntarily devoted an enormous amount of hours to help the NTCA evolve and move forward.

Additionally, I want to acknowledge all the members of the NTCA Throwers Hall of Fame. All of our Hall of Fame members have been immensely helpful in our endeavors. The encouragement and assistance from these distinguished people have been invaluable to this organization.

Of course, the core of the National Throws Coaches Association is its membership. Coaches, athletes, officials, and fans have made the NTCA into an exciting, respected, and highly viable coaching organization.

Finally, and most importantly, I would like to thank the co-founder of the National Coaches Throws Coaches Association: my wonderful wife, Mary Lasorsa. Simply put, without Mary, this organization would not exist. Her boundless energy and commitment of untold hours to the NTCA have had an invaluable impact on the organization.

— R.L.

Gary Aldrich
Associate head coach for the men's and women's track and field program at Carnegie Mellon University; vice president of the National Throws and Coaches Association; previously coached at Slippery Rock, Allegheny College, and Alfred University (head coach); lead instructor for Level I USA Track & Field Coaching Certification.

Duncan Atwood
Two-time U.S. Olympian in the javelin; one of the country's top throwers for over a decade; owner and founder of Pocket Videos, which is widely renowned for its technical flip books and sequence posters.

Mike Boyle, MA, CSCS, ATC
President of Elite Conditioning in Boston, MA; former head strength and conditioning coach at Boston University for 15 years; served as the strength and conditioning coach for the Boston Bruins of the National Hockey League; was the strength and conditioning coach for the 1998 US Women's Olympic ice hockey team; served as a consultant for the USA Hockey National Team Development Program.

Jeanmarie R. Burke
Dean of basic sciences and research at the New York Chiropractic College, as well as an associate professor of research in physiology of spinal manipulation; author of over 30 books; received the 2003 Faculty Award for Excellence in Research and Scholarly Activity at the NY Chiropractic College.

Jeff Chakouian
One of the most successful throwers in New England High School history; won five Massachusetts state champion titles and owns the state record shot-put throw of almost 68 feet; a five-time SEC champion and six-time All-American while attending the University of Kentucky.

Joe Donahue
Thirty-seventh season of coaching at Northeastern University; was the throwing coach at Northeastern from 1963-'99 and then rejoined the Northeastern staff in 2003; coached the only NCAA champion in any sport in Northeastern history, Boris Djerassi, who won the national hammer title in 1975, as well as many other All-Americans.

Bonnie Edmonson
Director of health education for the Connecticut State Department of Education; a trailblazer among women hammer throwers while at Eastern CT State University; served as USA Track & Field's women's hammer throw chairperson.

contributors

Matt Ellis
New England regional chairman for the National Throws Coaches Association; has worked for M-F Athletic Company for the past five years, specializing in all aspects of the throws; while employed at M-F Athletic Company, has spoken at numerous track and field clinics and coached at several track and field camps around the country.

Jim Giroux, CSCS
Has been with M-F Athletic Company/Perform Better for six years; previously coached track and field at UMass for 12 years; has USATF Level 2 certification, as well as CSCS certification through the NSCA.

Mark Harsha
Throws coach at Portage High School in Indiana; National Throws Coaches Association Indiana coordinator; founder of www.indianathrower.com website.

Larry W. Judge, Ph.D.
One of the most respected and successful throws coaches in the United States; college coaching experience includes Indiana State University, University of South Carolina, University of Wyoming (Head Coach), and University of Florida; serves as chair of USA Track and Field's Throws Coaches Certification program.

Rob Lasorsa
President and co-founder of the National Throws Coaches Association; has served as chair of men's shot development for USA Track and Field since 1994; previously, coaching stints at North Carolina State University, United States Military Academy, and Kent State University.

Chad Moreau, CSCS
Team strength and conditioning specialist for the ECHL's (formerly the East Coast Hockey League) Long Beach Ice Dogs; serves as a strength and conditioning consultant for the Edmonton Oilers hockey club; directs Back to Function, a sports chiropractic and strength and conditioning center in Lomita, CA.

Steve Myrland
Owner of Myrland Sports Training in Middleton, WI; formerly on the strength and conditioning staff at University of Wisconsin; designed the ABC Agility Ladder.

Joe Napoli
National Throws Coaches Association Mid-Atlantic and New Jersey coordinator; currently, throws coach at Howell High School (NJ); tremendous athlete under the tutelage of Al Schoterman at Kent State University in the 1980s.

James A. Peterson, Ph.D., FACSM
Former faculty member at the United States Military Academy at West Point; currently, a sports medicine consultant who resides in Monterey, California; author of over 80 books and 200 published articles.

Tom Pukstys
Six-time U.S. javelin champion; 2-time Olympian; ranked #1 in U.S. seven times by *Track and Field News*; currently, USA Track and Field men's javelin department chair; president of TP Sports.

Robb Rogers, M.Ed, CSCS, MSCC
Performance coach, St. Vincent Sports Performance in Indianapolis; has coached athletes of every level; has worked on the strength and conditioning staffs at the University of Missouri, USC, Baylor University, and the St. Louis Blues of the National Hockey League.

Mohamad Saatara
Coaches the throws, vertical jumps, and multi-event athletes at Northern Arizona University; in his first three seasons at NAU, has coached 16 All Big Sky Conference athletes (indoor and outdoor), including indoor men's and women's weight throw, hammer throw, and shot put Big Sky Conference Champions; previously, served as the head track and field coach at California State at Los Angeles.

Al Schoterman
Former American record holder and Olympian in the hammer; NCAA record holder; as the throws coach at Kent State University, produced numerous All-Americans and one American record holder (Jud Logan).

Paul E. Turner, Ph.D.
Enters his 13th season at Harvard, following successful stints at Indiana University and Western Michigan University; has coached numerous US and foreign national team members, most recently Irish Olympic discus thrower Nick Sweeney and Jamaican national team hammer thrower Nicky Grant; in addition, has coached several collegians who have attained All-American status, including Harvard javelin thrower Chris Clever.

Bruce Van Horne
Vice-president of the National Throws Coaches Association; highly successful high school coach at Blackhawk High School (PA) for 23 years; much sought-after clinician and speaker.

Mike Young
Coach for the Army's men's sprint team and the owner of Human Performance Consulting; currently serves as the biomechanics chair for USATF's Coaches Education Division and is one of only three coaches to be a Level 3 instructor in both the jumps and throws; for the past five years, has served as the shot put biomechanist for USA Track and Field's high performance division, where he has worked closely with several of America's best athletes.

contents

As an experienced athlete, I had the opportunity to compete against many of the world's top throwers during my career. Among the many things I learned is that there is no shortcut for hard work. The simple truth of the matter is that good coaching will bring out the best in those athletes who are willing to work hard. I also learned that it's often too easy to fall into the trap that somehow a magic recipe for success exists. In reality, there is no substitute for superior training, sound technique, and quality coaching.

My experience has shown that the athletes who consistently perform the best are those who have learned, often through trial and error, how to adhere to proper technique and suitable training for their event. Those who try training short-cuts, by following the latest fad or other unproven methods, rarely live up to their potential. In fact, the over-reliance on these alternative approaches and problems typically results in performance problems, more often than not...unable to achieve meaningful improvement, unable to address the deficiencies in their technique, and unable to maximize their God-given talent.

The *2007 NTCA Throws Handbook* provides a wealth of information for coaches who want to help their throwers perform at their best. The 34 articles included in this book represent some of the best and brightest minds in the track and field community. The compilation of articles in this book addresses a comprehensive array of topics, ranging from both essential coaching guidelines and specific technical instruction in the five throws events to basic information on sports physiology and biomechanics. Collectively, the articles are designed to help coaches and athletes at all competitive levels.

The editing combination of a respected coach and a sports medicine consultant couldn't be better, as they integrate the critically important aspects of their knowledge base into this exceptional collection of articles. If you're a coach and want to know proper training guidelines, this book is for you. Lasorsa and Peterson have put together a helpful text that is easy to use, easy to access, and easy to understand. It's a book that I enthusiastically recommend to all coaches and athletes who want to maximize their abilities.

> — Randy Matson
> 1968 Olympic Gold Medalist in the shot put;
> first individual to throw the shot over 70'

Foreword

1

Coaching the Hammer When You Have Never Coached It Before

By Gary Aldrich

What do you do when you have never coached the hammer before, and you are now at a school where they throw the hammer? Well, the first thing I did was to call Jud Logan to get ideas and feedback from him. The next thing I did was read and watched videos on the event. John Copeland's *Come to Hammer Practice* from M-F Athletic Co. gave me several basic drills to use.

Where do you actually start when teaching the hammer? The first factor you must consider is the need to be aware of the tremendous need for safety. The main concern of all throwing events should be the safety of the athletes and spectators. Never forget or become complacent about this factor, for this is when accidents are most likely to happen.

> The main concern of all throwing events should be the safety of the athletes and spectators.

Mechanically, I start with the thrower's stance. His knees need to be flexed with his hips and shoulders over his heels. His head should be up with his eyes focusing on the horizon. His hands should form a grip, which will allow his arms to form a triangle. For a right-handed thrower, the thrower should hold the hammer handle in his left hand (which is why a right-handed thrower needs a left-handed glove) with the first digits. The right hand should be laid on top, with the thumbs together, similar to a bumping-hand position in volleyball. The thrower should be sure not to let his thumbs cross.

Once the thrower has a balanced starting position and grip, we can work on his winds—the action that initiates the hammer moving in an orbit around the thrower. Again, as a right-handed thrower, we start with the ball on the right side of the thrower and behind. I used the cues *push, curl, comb,* and *turn*. The thrower should push the ball with his right side. The big mistake throwers will make in this instance is they will pull with their left side. Once the hands get to around 11:00 (reference point: 12:00 is at the back of the circle, and 6:00 is at the front of the circle where the thrower will release the hammer), the thrower should curl his hands toward his head. The back of the right hand acts as if he were combing his hair. He should make sure that his elbows stay in front. When winding the ball, his head and shoulders should turn to catch the ball on recovery to the right side.

Once the thrower has completed two winds, you will want your athlete to initiate the turns.

Once the thrower has completed two winds, you will want your athlete to initiate the turns. The turns are started with the thrower's feet. The left foot will pivot on the heel to 8:00, while at the same time, the right foot is pivoting on the ball of the foot. Do not let the knees separate. An excellent drill in this instance is to place a slightly deflated volleyball between the knees and try to pivot. If the knees separate, the ball will fall to the ground. Once the thrower gets to the 8:00 position, he should step his right foot over his left foot. It is important that the right foot does not circle—it steps over. It also allows the athlete to get back to a double-support position as quickly as possible. This allows for better balance and a better ability to push the ball around, rather than pulling it or letting it drag behind. Both feet should pivot on the balls of the feet to a 12:00 position. The athlete has now completed one turn. One drill that allowed my athletes to really work on this action was to hold a folding chair by the legs and do the turn in phases: 1) pivot on the heel of the left and ball of the right; pause; 2) step over the left with the right; pause; and then 3) pivot on both feet on the balls, back to 12:00.

Once the thrower has achieved a balanced starting position and a proper grip, the next step is to work on the thrower's winds.

Michael Steele/Getty Images Sport

Again, quite possibly because I was not a hammer thrower and didn't have much experience with it, I made my athletes really work and understand one turn before proceeding to two and three turns. Some coaches may have their athletes move right into utilizing three turns. Such an approach was hard for me, because I was learning what to look for and what to see. In my opinion, having my athletes work on turn one allowed them to be in a better position to move into turn two, and then turn three. As a result, they developed a better understanding of how to achieve the rhythm essential to throwing the hammer.

Among the drills that I employed to get my athletes used to moving with the ball were the following:

Having my athletes work on turn one allowed them to be in a better position to move into turn two, and then turn three.

- Hands out, straight walk around turns, not using a hammer, while maintaining a good triangle position with the arms.
- Hands out, with a hammer or other weight, maybe a shot put. Walk around, but increase the tempo as the turns increase.
- Walk around, concentrating on hitting a low point at 1:00 and a high point at 8:00.
- Walk around, hitting the low point and the high point, and then release.
- Grip the hammer in the right hand and then wind. This drill is designed to develop the concept of pushing the ball.
- Grip the right forearm with the left hand and do a wind. This starts to develop the sensation of having two arms and hands on the implement.
- Two-handed winds.
- Two-handed winds, and then walk around turns.
- Two winds, and then walk around, hitting the low and the high points.
- Two winds, then walk around, hitting the low and the high points, and then release.
- Walk along a line on your left heel and right toe.
- Stand on a line with your left foot; pivot 180 degrees on the heel of your left foot and the ball of your right foot. Repeat.
- Stand on a line with your left foot; pivot 180 degrees on the heel of your left foot and the ball of your right foot; hold the ball of the hammer with your right hand and put the left hand on your hip. Repeat.
- Holding the hammer properly with just the right hand, have the ball on the ground, and pivot on your heel and toe, keeping the ball rolling on the ground.
- Roll the hammer on the ground with the normal grip. Do three turns.
- Roll the hammer on the ground with the normal grip. Do three turns, but allow the hammer to rise above the ground.
- Do three turns, keeping the hammer on a flat orbit.
- Two winds, three turns—achieve a high and a low point.

- Two winds, one turn, and then release.
- Two winds, two or three turns, and then release.

Finally, some key points to remember:

- Push the ball; don't pull it.
- Don't pull the left side or the head away too soon.
- During release, keep the feet pivoting until the knees touch, then explode, and lift.
- Keep the hammer in line with the triangle that your arms form.

Good luck. I became very excited about teaching the hammer. I learned and developed a great appreciation for a tremendous event.

2

Progressions for Obtaining a Proper Power Position in the Shot Put or Discus

By Gary Aldrich

Start by getting in a toe-heel relationship with your feet. For a right-handed thrower, the toe of the left foot (blocking foot) should be aligned with the heel of the right foot (throwing foot). The feet should be approximately shoulder-width apart.

What I like young throwers to do next is to rock back and forth, shifting their weight from the right foot to the left foot. As the thrower is rocking, let him lift the non-supporting foot off the ground. This action will allow for a great shift in his weight. It will also teach him about transferring his weight from one side of the body to the other. After rocking for a number of times, when he shifts his weight to his throwing foot, hold that position. What has occurred is all the weight is now back on the throwing foot side. Then rock again. Then hold the weight. Make sure when he holds the weight back, that he can lift the blocking foot off the ground.

Now, with the weight back on the throwing side of the body, bend the throwing knee. This movement allows the thrower to get to a lower level. A common mistake that occurs in this instance is that the thrower will allow his weight to shift to the middle of both feet. The blocking knee will also bend. What you should see is the weight back on and over the throwing side and the blocking leg straight. The reason for a knee bend is because the implement is thrown with the legs. The legs, lower back, and buttocks are much stronger than the arm. To utilize these muscle groups, the thrower must go from a low

The reason for a knee bend is because the implement is thrown with the legs.

level to a high level (i.e., bending of the knee to straightening of the knee). This lifting action will give us the thrower height at release.

The next action is to give a quarter turn to the throwing side with the upper body. This turn loads the implement behind the throwing hip. Make sure that when the athlete turns that he does not tilt his shoulders. The shoulders should stay parallel to the ground. If the athlete has limited flexibility in the abdomen area, it will be very difficult for the athlete to turn and load the implement. This loading allows for an increase in torque on the body, which will, when released, add more force to the throw. A straight line should exist from the blocking toe through the body to the head of the thrower. The thrower should look like a ski jumper going off the 90-meter hill.

If the athlete has limited flexibility in the abdomen area, it will be very difficult for the athlete to turn and load the implement.

Andy Lyons/Getty Images Sport

3

Glide Shot Put Coaches Can Coach the Rotational Shot Technique

By Gary Aldrich and Bruce Van Horne

It seems as though every clinic we speak at we are asked, "Is it hard to teach the rotational technique to shot putters?" or "How do you determine which thrower you should teach to spin in the shot put?" The answers to these questions are "no" and "it depends."

"Is it hard to teach the rotational technique in the shot put?" It is interesting that we get this question asked as often as we do. The majority of coaches that ask this question coach their throwers in both the shot put and discus. So, they already do teach the rotational technique to their discus throwers. But for some reason, they are not sure how to communicate the technique to their shot putters.

The rotational technique for the discus and shot put is very similar, although a few differences exist. Hopefully, by highlighting these subtle differences, it will make teaching the technique less stressful. The first difference that we talk about is the body position at the back of the circle (reference point: 12:00 is the back of the circle; 6:00 is at the toe board. It should also be noted that this article is written in terms of a right-handed thrower).

The rotational technique for the discus and shot put is very similar.

The starting position for the SP (shot put) is a slight, more forward bend at the waist, with the chest being closer in distance to the quads. This position is similar to a semi-squat position. Coaches also sometimes see the placement of the shot being back behind the ear. You have to be careful with this. Much

Andy Lyons/Getty Images Sport

It is not overly difficult for glide shot put coaches to
teach the rotational shot technique.

of the reason for this placement is the size of the 16-pound shot when looking at film of elite throwers. Women/girls and high school boys do not need to place the shot that far back because of the size of the shot. They can handle the ball. The tendency is if the ball is too far back in the neck, the right elbow will get in front of the ball and not allow for an advantageous pushing position.

Because the shot circle is seven feet in diameter, while the discus circle is eight feet, two and a half inches, the right knee must lift more in the shot put as opposed to driving across the circle in the discus.

The next difference involves the wind of the rotational shot versus the discus. The load in the shot should just be enough to load the ball behind the right hip. The final difference is the driving of the right knee across the circle. Because the shot circle is seven feet in diameter, while the discus circle is eight feet, two and a half inches, the right knee must lift more in the shot put as opposed to driving across the circle in the discus. This factor is especially true if you have a tall thrower. It is very easy for a thrower six feet, six inches tall to get across a shot put circle. So much so, that if the thrower doesn't lift the knee, the thrower will be very crowded at the toe board. There are other differences, but if you work on these, it will get your throwers into a better position to deliver the ball.

"How do you determine which thrower you should teach to spin in the shot put?" The first thing you should look at is, do your throwers look and feel comfortable in spinning in the discus? Are they fluid and move smoothly through the circle, or are they very mechanical and choppy? This factor also applies to whether they have good feet.

In other words, are they mobile, athletic, and on their toes? Can they be active and coordinated? If they have these traits, it will make it much easier to teach the proper movement patterns for the rotational shot technique. On the other hand, this doesn't mean that once you are a glider you are always a glider. Remember, athletes mature and develop at different rates. Some freshmen can walk and talk at the same time. Others can't. But by the time they are all seniors, however, they are typically able to move in any direction and in any way you want them to move.

In fact, a number of throwers have gone from being good gliding shot putters to excellent rotating shot putters, for example, Jeff Chakouian—a shot putter at the University of Kentucky. Jeff was a glide shot putter out of Massachusetts who, as a senior in high school, was one of the best in the nation. His coach at UK, John Kenneson, decided to teach Jeff the rotational technique as soon as he came to Kentucky. John's decision was a success right from the get-go. Jeff threw over 20 meters in his first meet. Obviously, that type of success will not happen for everyone. The point is that a coach cannot be afraid to try something different if he thinks it will make his throwers better.

The other aspect of the athlete that we encourage coaches to look at is the emotional stability of their throwers. Are their athletes able to handle adversity and respond well, as opposed to getting depressed and pouting? The reason why this factor is important is because the rotational technique can be very erratic. The glide technique is much more consistent. The deviation between throws, if they were to be plotted, is not as great in the glide compared to the rotational. Therefore, a rotational thrower must be able to handle not succeeding well on the first and maybe even the second throw. Eventually, the thrower will be able to pull it all together on the third.

A rotational thrower must be able to handle not succeeding well on the first and maybe even the second throw.

No matter which technique you teach your shot putters to use, you should be confident and positive. Continue to develop your knowledge. You should also encourage your athletes to attend clinics, read, and/or watch videos and DVDs. The effort will enable your throwers and programs to flourish.

4

After the Release– Javelin Follow-Through Tips

By Duncan Atwood

The follow-through in the javelin can really tell a story. Great throws (not only for the javelin but on other throws as well) can show the observer whether the *momentum, balance, timing,* and *steps* were attended to or not. On quality throws, there is often a vault up and over the plant leg, with the non-plant leg taking a giant step up and forward. This action is sometimes called "stepping over the post." Exceptions exist, from Al Cantello (a nose-diver) to Jan Zelezny (nose dives, multiple steps, face plants, and others), but this article will discuss elements of more typically seen techniques.

Momentum

A big difference between great throwers and not-so-great ones is the amount of distance covered in the crossover, plant, and follow-through steps.

Since better throws occur *during acceleration* in the run, rather than as the athlete is slowing down, there's momentum to arrest before the line. Too often, advancing throwers will get too close to the foul line because they are moving faster (finally) down the runway. The next change should be to move the step back, so the throw can be attacked without going over the line. But, typically, throwers will either try to stop quicker or simply slow down their approach. Both are mistakes. Crowding the line means the steps need to go back, even if it's really far back. A big difference between great throwers and not-so-great ones is the amount of distance covered in the crossover, plant, and follow-through steps. These last few steps eat up a lot of ground and must be allowed to do so. Reducing momentum during the throw to help avoid fouling is the opposite of what the thrower should be doing; yet, it is common. So, keep or increase the momentum; the evidence of this will be a more active follow-through that uses up more distance.

Balance

The typical beginner throws off balance, after tilting forward off of a straight non-plant leg. The resulting follow-through is a break forward at the waist and a lot of arm waving to keep balance. This situation occurs because the center of momentum is about at chest level, rather than at the hip level in the more advanced thrower. The following example illustrates this point: if you're standing straight up on a skateboard going 10 mph and you step off, your upper body will be flung forward, and you might not be able to keep your balance. Solution: slow down, right? Wrong. Lean back instead, and lower yourself by bending your knees, then look down your nose, but with the head tilted back. Now, as you step off, your hips and lower torso will vault upwards, and you'll take a big, big step and arrive reasonably vertical as you stop.

The typical beginner throws off balance, after tilting forward off of a straight non-plant leg.

Timing

Bad timing can put a thrower off balance, so the follow-through results can look the same. However, timing problems (e.g., typically waiting too long on the non-plant leg) can be helped by exaggerating the rhythm until the problems become obvious. A thrower may suffer an especially jolting follow-through because of bad timing as well.

Mike Powell/Getty Images Sport

The follow-through in the javelin can really tell a story.

Steps

Getting consistent with the steps (and therefore the run-up) can really help the follow-through. But, this doesn't mean keeping the distances of the start and drawback points the same. Keep the number of steps and crossovers consistent, trying extra steps or crossovers, and removing extra steps or crossovers, until the throw is reasonably predictable. By getting consistent, the run can be examined and pieces adjusted without having to start over all the time. Precisely adjusting the speed of the run is a huge issue as well. Most throwers alter their run-up speed too much—try to add or subtract speed, just a little at a time. Otherwise, it's too hard to tell what's happening. When the steps are on, the follow-through is smooth, and there may be as much as a meter or two at the line. When you're really good (and lucky), you stop closer. It also gets closer when you're struggling, usually cutting off the throw, so you don't go flying over the line.

Most good throwers routinely go over the line, sometimes by as much as two meters.

In training, most good throwers routinely go over the line, sometimes by as much as two meters. This way, they can follow-through to their heart's content, and the throws are better. Subsequently, they are able to move their steps back and keep to the same number of steps for meets. Gaining this ability can really help a thrower. Recently, I read some javelin training material from the 1930s, which advised hurdling to help gain proficiency in stride count and tempo. This point really hit home with me, as I ran 400m hurdles (slowly: 59.6) for exactly this reason. More realistically, four hurdles spaced for the 400 and run as repeats is a better use of energy. Getting 17 steps, then 15, can make a thrower fluent in the footwork needed to control the run-up.

The next time you look at javelin videos, check out the follow-through. You may see something telling about the throw. Something odd—after the momentum has gone, sometimes from a complete standstill, many throwers will raise their arms in the direction of the throw. Part of the rhythm? Avoiding a walk-over foul? Throwers have unique individual patterns.

5

Coaching Beginning Javelin Throwers

By Duncan Atwood

Every year, I encounter the complete newcomer to the javelin and the conversations usually go like this:

"Let's see, you throw it kind of like a baseball, right?" No! A baseball is *round*; a javelin is straight. The path of the hand in a baseball throw is an arc, with the release at the top of the arc. The path of the hand in a javelin throw is straight, with the release at the end of the straight path. The baseball tumbles as it flies—the javelin must fly straight. Football throwing for distance is far more similar to javelin throwing because of the football's lengthwise axis, but the emphasis on accuracy brings the focus of the throw to the arm, which causes other problems.

"Gosh, this thing is light. I bet I could throw it a mile." Both statements are incorrect. High school and international men's javelins weigh 800 grams—women's are 600. That's equal to 9.2 baseballs for the men's and 6.9 for the women's javelins. Baseballs weighing 800 or 600 grams often bring this reaction: "Wow, this is heavy. I could hurt my arm throwing this." The javelin's weight *for its size* may create a deception of lightness, but the ligaments and tendons of the elbow and shoulder are not deceived.

> The javelin's weight for its size may create a deception of lightness, but the ligaments and tendons of the elbow and shoulder are not deceived.

"Throw it with my legs?" "How can running up help?" More trouble. The idea of using the body's momentum to launch something is not the first thing a novice visualizes, but it can be developed. Fortunately, most athletes can imagine how running up to kick a ball adds distance to the kick, and the javelin run-up works in a similar way.

Because of these factors, we need to teach the beginner a completely new kind of throwing. The following easy drills can help get the beginner looking for parts of the throw that can be developed to produce greater distance:

☐ *Alignment and walking.* The javelin should be thrown straight. Walk up and down the throwing field holding the javelin, and gently toss the implement, while walking and continuing to walk (so as to include a follow-through step). The throws should be 10-to-20 yards, go through a nice arc, and land directly on the point at about 30-to-40 degrees. Most beginners need about three days of half an hour each day before they can reliably do 10 in a row. Just holding both arms up will be tiring. Doing this drill along a field sideline (if available) to keep the walking and throwing lined up is also useful.

Beginners must learn to lean back (in the direction of the javelin tail, not toward their non-facing side; see arms up and lean) to add leverage to their throws.

☐ *Add lean back and skipping.* Beginners must learn to lean back (in the direction of the javelin tail, not toward their non-facing side) to add leverage to their throws. The lean comes both from the torso bent behind the hips and from tilting the hips. It's quite unnatural for beginners, but vital to learn. The change from walking to skipping gives the thrower the idea of putting a more ballistic bounce into the throw and the timing required to do it. Holding the javelin with both arms up, the athlete simply skips in a sideways version of very standard forward skipping. It's very important that the skipping include a follow-through step. The distances thrown for this drill range from 15-to-30 yards. There should be no effort from the arm. Add to all this the arcing flight that lands squarely on the point, and your thrower will be busy for hours trying to get it right.

☐ *Speed it up.* Skipping onto the throw gives the feeling of how to put running energy into a throw. This is fine, but skipping is limited with the speed it can generate, so now a run must be added. Like a run to kick a ball, a beginning javelin run starts slowly and builds with each step into the skip/leap/crossover into the throw. Many coaches and throwers aren't sure how many crossovers to use. The answer is as many crossovers as the athlete feels is needed to "get ready" for the throw, usually one-to-three. If a thrower wants more, it's usually because he isn't preparing sufficiently for the throw with his upper body. Another key point to focus on in the last steps is to try to remain low to the ground; again, as in kicking, the dynamics of force transfer (and adding to that force) become impossible if the thrower leaps too high.

Many successful throwers started out like this and simply practiced these simple ideas until they could run faster and faster into the throw without losing balance and keeping the javelin flying well. Once the first year is over, workouts should be long and focused. It takes a while to "get into it," and once there, the athlete should be sufficiently conditioned to having 30-to-60 throws, jogging to retrieve the thrown javelins, and then having the best throws of the session take place near the end of the workout.

In reality, most javelin beginners aren't able to maintain the proper technique, not so much because they don't understand it, but because their bodies aren't prepared for this unusual motion. In this regard, the following simple conditioning tricks can make a difference:

☐ *Arms up.* Holding a javelin in the throwing hand, have the athlete hold both arms and shoulders high and take big walking crossover steps around the track.

CHAPTER FIVE

Beginners usually don't last 75m before the arms come down. Intervals are OK (e.g., 5 x 50m). In a throwing workout, keeping the arms high really helps.

☐ *Low-heel-toe*. As mentioned earlier, staying low in the throw can eliminate a number of problems. However, most beginners aren't strong in a low position. This drill can be very tiring, but effective, for building strength in this position. Again, holding the javelin in throwing position with the arms high, have the athlete look in the direction of the throw and squat down until the thighs are almost parallel to the ground. Using a crab-like motion, quickly bring the toe of the rear foot to the heel of the front foot and repeat (and repeat and repeat for about 50m). This drill really targets the quadriceps of the rear leg (the right leg on a right-handed thrower) and should be done almost as a series of one-legged hops. Athletes not in shape sometimes don't last 20m, so have them do something like 8 x 10m (heel-toe sequence).

Most beginners aren't strong in a low position.

☐ *Look out the bottom of your face*. This drill involves easy throwing (four steps, then skip, then throw and follow through, about 20-to-30m, with good solid point hits) with the head tilted back so the thrower is viewing the target (e.g., cloud, tree, etc., at about 30 degrees up) down along the face, as if to peek from under a pair of glasses. This drill is designed to train the skill of throwing from a leaning back position (the "backward C") and condition the athlete in this position. Twenty-to-30 easy throws should be OK at first (later up to 100 of these), while jogging up and down the field, can be great for advanced high school and college throwers.

Matthew Stockman/Getty Images Sport

The javelin run-up works in a way similar to running up to kick a ball.

Other great conditioners include running sprints such as 200m or 400m hurdle straight-aways, lots of stretching, and some mild gymnastics. The usual medicine ball and weightlifting exercises work too, but beginners need to focus on dynamic specifics for the event. Another effective option is to perform lots of throwing (not using the arm), while practicing the aforementioned points and making sure the javelin flies and lands correctly. Above all, have fun.

6

Developing a Javelin Run-Up

By Duncan Atwood

Developing the run-up in the javelin can be a struggle. Done well, the run-up can add up to 80 feet to a throw. Done poorly, a full run can subtract distance from a three- or five-step approach. Many coaches and athletes deal with this issue by throwing from a short run most of the time, and then hoping it solves itself when the season arrives. Sometimes it does, usually it doesn't.

The key is to think of the javelin run-up as being an amped-up version of the run-up used to kick a ball for distance. Both runs accelerate, both require a predictable number of steps so as to arrive at the ball or scratch line without overstepping, both have a rhythm with a final leap into the plant, both add power to the kick or throw, and both result in a follow-through. This comparison is useful because most athletes and coaches have enough experience with kicking to get the idea. Few have seen many good javelin run-ups, and even fewer have done it themselves.

Many styles exist for making the run-up effective. To allow for this, a system for developing the run-up should include "athlete determined" aspects of the run, such as the number of steps, rhythm pattern, and overall length of the run. As with the ball kick, the javelin run needs to be automatic enough to allow the athlete to hold the sense of the throw in mind during the run-up rather than, for example, watching for the scratch line. The athlete must be confident that the run will truly contribute to the throw, or bad things can happen at meets.

The following steps offer an effective approach for developing the javelin run-up:

Select an unmarked grass field. In the beginning, extra steps are necessary, and a grass field eliminates scratch line apprehension and worries about distance. Make sure the spikes are long enough. After a good warm-up and stretch, have the athlete stand with the javelin already withdrawn, and mark the spot.

> The key is to think of the javelin run-up as being an amped-up version of the run-up used to kick a ball for distance.

The run-up should be a build-up like that of a ball kick or long jump.

Have the athlete run up and throw. The run-up should be a build-up like that of a ball kick or long jump. Your athletes usually ease into something like a final crossover. If necessary, acquaint them with the basics—upper body sideways for a few steps, with the lower body working to a final crossover and plant. Do not throw hard. Mark the spot where they come to a stop after the throw. This point is their temporary scratch line. Also mark the landing point of the javelin. This step is not to later measure the best throw, but to provide feedback about how effective the run-ups are relative to each other. Move the mark to the farthest throw of the day. It can be exciting for an athlete to experience easy throws going farther than hard ones. If possible, set it up so that there is no objective knowledge of the distance, so experimentation is easier.

It is worth repeating that the run-up should power the throw; the idea is to get throws that increase in distance because of increasing the speed of the run-up, as the athlete continues to report very little throwing effort. A quality flight is also important, as is the plant. Those are big topics in themselves, but sometimes they happen naturally, if the run-up is in order.

Briefly, the javelin should fly at about 30-to-35 degrees, and the plant needs to hit heel first with the leg at about a 50-degree angle. A slight knee bend is OK; a major bend is not. Post up and over the plant into the follow-through.

Stu Forster/Getty Images Sport

Many styles exist for making the run-up effective.

While the path of the throwing arm is often the topic of much discussion, it is almost completely a function of the run-up. Furthermore, most arm problems, in both mechanical-efficiency and injury areas, can be traced to the run-up.

Repeat as many times as it takes for the athlete to become consistent with the number of steps taken. Keep the start point the same, but move the scratch line as necessary. The javelin landing-point mark should be moved each time as well. This endeavor helps the athlete gain a sense of what's working and what isn't. The throws should be very light, with the emphasis on smoothness, continuity of the run into the throw, and ease of throwing effort.

Once the steps are consistent, the coach needs to count them, noting how many crossovers have been chosen. Because most throwing coaches don't have much experience counting steps, they don't value this element of coaching, but it's critical. The javelin is a runway event first and a throw second. You can be sure that in the other runway events, very careful attention to step counting is basic.

Because most throwing coaches don't have much experience counting steps, they don't value this element of coaching, but it's critical.

The next throwing session picks up where the last one left off. It is a big mistake to allow random run-ups to the scratch line, guessing at the start point, and blowing over the line by 10 feet. Still, on the unmarked field, the athlete needs to establish the "rhythm of the day" (hopefully not too different from the previous session, although it can vary widely in the beginning), establish a start point and stick to it, and repeat step three, striving for consistency, while keeping a smooth, building run-up.

After perhaps five sessions of starting with the javelin already withdrawn and seeing that some consistency has been reliably established with the number of steps to the throw, try establishing an initial start point about 20-to-30 feet back from the original start point. The athlete should now begin the run facing forward, with the throwing hand roughly by the head and the javelin flat, to see if a drawback at the old start point can be established. This undertaking may require several sessions to reestablish the steps. Now that there is speed into what was a static start point, the scratch line will probably have to be moved, perhaps up to 10 feet further down the field.

Other elements to vary are speed and rhythm. Speed changes need to be very incremental—if the changes are too large, it's too hard to sort out what's going on. Add speed until the control suffers; back off in tiny amounts until control returns. Then add speed in small amounts again until control is a struggle, and then back off again. Repeating this process helps the athlete learn how the run-up speed influences the throw. Rhythm changes can occur spontaneously. Once I had an athlete say that he felt like he needed to add a small, quick step before going into his final crossover. He was able to test it effectively because his steps were consistent. It worked for him by giving him a better sense of the timing of the throw. A coach can suggest a change such as this, but knowing what's going to work is trial and mostly error.

Don't forget the follow-through. As the run-up speed improves, the follow-through should lengthen. Allow this. In fact, if the follow-through is short after a long, fast run, it's a sign of slowing down during the throw. The throw takes place during a *run*, not during a *stop*. The follow-through can be two or even three steps long. Practice,

As throwers improve, their stride length will increase to a point where the same number of steps doesn't fit on the runway.

practice, practice. In maybe 10-to-15 sessions, the athlete should begin to establish a decent run-up that can be tinkered with without having to start over. As throwers improve, their stride length will increase to a point where the same number of steps doesn't fit on the runway. Just move the checkpoints back. I've seen throwers be uncertain about moving their steps back as much as two javelin lengths in a meet when they're psyched and blowing over the line. Move the start point back *three* lengths, if necessary.

To back up this development, javelin throwers need to R-U-N. I try to get my athletes to build up to five-to-ten times 60m of crossovers with the javelin. They need 10m to get going, 15m to have a few bad ones, another 15m to figure it out (or I yell at them what to fix), and then maybe 20m to have a good series before tiring. They need to learn to run *fast* with floating steps, while holding the javelin *back* and *steady*. It's harder than most coaches and athletes realize, but it does respond well to actually practicing it. Add a backward lean, and it really is a special skill. All the top javelin throwers make it look easy, which it is if you practice, but not, if you don't.

The running crossovers also go a long way to strengthening the adductor (groin) muscles, which are easily strained in javelin throwers. Additional specific strength is gained in holding the arms up while running with a torso twist. Although these aspects of strength are vital to a comfortable run-up, they aren't developed in the weight room.

Additional steps that can be employed to help develop an effective javelin run-up include:

☐ *Practice hurdling.* Set up four intermediate height (or lower, if needed) hurdles down the backstretch. Have the thrower run over them, counting their steps. Maybe they'll take 15 if they are runners; maybe they'll take 21 if they aren't. No matter—it's great for conditioning and to learn how to count steps. The leap over the hurdle is like a crossover in the effort made to spring off the ground, and landing running is like the landing after the crossover—the athlete must keep moving into the throw. Javelin throwers should learn to hurdle, alternating the lead leg; this action creates a skilled, flexible, dynamic lower body, so often lacking in javelin throwers. Make it easy at first.

☐ *Practice skipping.* In Finland, children (most of whom are already familiar with skipping) are taught the run-up by skipping with the javelin and trying to put the skip into the throw. Like a crow hop in baseball, but with more momentum, skipping into the throw is an easy way for beginners to feel how to put a hop (the precursor to the crossover) into the throw. It is essential that any throw include a follow-through. Again, the kick analogy is appropriate. The final leap the kicker makes into the kick is like the skip or crossover into the throw and a good long kick always has a natural follow-through.

Start with continuous sideways skipping, holding the javelin in a drawn-back position. Use the non-throwing arm to help balance and amplify the skip. It may take a few practices to get control of the point while skipping. Make sure it is done while leaning back along the shaft of the javelin. Then add a short toss as the athlete is landing from a skip. Make sure that the throw involves virtually no effort and that the javelin flies through the point. After that is consistent (30+ good flights), the thrower can move to running into the skip with an easy toss. The run can be facing forward, crossovers, or in between—it's the skip and timing of the throw that count.

☐ *Exaggerate the rhythm.* Add moments of hang time, quick bursts of legwork, and anything you can think of to get the athlete to add rhythm to the throw. The best run-ups have noticeable breaks in the continuity of the run worked into an overall smoothness.

☐ *Don't forget the left arm (or right arm for you lefties).* By being active, the non-throwing arm can really help to balance and smooth things out.

☐ *Remember that the javelin starts flying as soon as the thrower starts down the runway.* Each step of the run-up needs to contribute to the smooth flight of the javelin. When this factor is done well, throwers report that all they did was run up and let it go. It's usually the farthest throw of the day.

By training the run-up the way the other runway events do, (i.e., by having a consistent start, check, and finish point), the javelin thrower can add huge distance and improve consistency. When throwers are confident that they won't run out of room at the line, they can attack the throw, follow-through, and then wait for the big number to come up on the board.

When throwers are confident that they won't run out of room at the line, they can attack the throw, follow through, and then wait for the big number to come up on the board.

7

Medicine Ball Training for Throwers

By Michael Boyle

Power development for throwers is often limited to Olympic lifting and plyometric drills. In recent years, medicine ball training has made a comeback to become an integral part of training for any athlete interested in power development. The development of a wide range of both elastic and non-elastic medicine balls has re-popularized a long lost technique. For throwers, the opportunity to develop rotational power is the primary benefit of medicine ball training. With both plyometrics and Olympic lifting, power development is uni-planar with no trunk focus. Medicine balls can be a tool like Olympic lifting and plyometrics for the trunk musculature. I often tell our athletes and coaches to think of medicine ball training as Olympic lifting for the core. The medicine ball, as a tool for power development, is unparalleled. No other training mode provides the specific strength and power potential of the medicine ball. Rotational medicine ball throws are the key to developing torso power for athletes involved in the throws. The new rubber medicine balls, combined with a masonry wall, are excellent for these applications, because of the elasticity of the ball.

> For overhead athletes, like the javelin thrower, the medicine ball provides great eccentric training for the rotator cuff, while developing power in the core muscles.

For overhead athletes, like the javelin thrower, the medicine ball provides great eccentric training for the rotator cuff, while developing power in the core muscles. In addition, for all throwers, total-body power can be developed through total-body throws with heavy balls. Total-body throws should be done in a large open area and are great to simulate the actions of the Olympic lifts. Total-body throws are particularly useful for coaches who do not feel comfortable teaching Olympic lifts. Balls like the Dynamax™ ball and the D-Balls are excellent for these applications, because they do not bounce. The Dynamax™ balls are also great for exercises like medicine ball bench presses. Medicine ball bench presses are excellent for upper-body power for larger athletes, since they do not stress the rotator cuff and shoulder like plyometric pushups and other bodyweight upper-body plyometrics. Furthermore, Dynamax™ ball can also be caught with minimal stresses on the wrists, due to its soft feel.

The Limit to the Medicine Ball is the Limit of the Coaches' Imagination

For rotational throws, it is best to find an area with a masonry wall. In rotational throws, the athlete can throw as hard as possible against the wall with balls in the four-to-five kilo range to develop true power in the core and hips. Excellent imitative drills for throwers can be developed once the athlete masters the basics.

For rotational throws, it is best to find an area with a masonry wall.

Rotation Progression

The rotational progression begins with the athlete on both knees in what is called a "tall-kneeling" position. Tall kneeling is a position with the athlete kneeling and the hips extended. Beginning with kneeling eliminates involving the ankle and knee joints and exposes weaknesses and compensation patterns that may not be visible in standing throws. In addition, "tall kneeling" teaches the athlete to use the glutes. For rotational exercises, use heavier balls to force the core to work. Adult males can start with four-to-five kilo balls. Among the positions that the athlete can employ in a rotation progression are the following:

1. *Kneeling front twist.* Facing the wall, two-to-three feet away.

2. *Kneeling side twist.* Ninety degrees to the wall, two-to-three feet away.

3. *Half-kneeling.* Front and side. Half-kneeling is a one knee-down position. These throws can de done with the inside knee up or down.

Tony Duffy/Getty Images Sport

I often tell our athletes and coaches to think of medicine ball training as Olympic lifting for the core.

4. *Lunge position.* Involves the same throws as the previous positions. Throwing from the lunge position challenges stability, strength, and flexibility. In addition, throwing from the lunge position develops isometric strength. Lunge position throws may, in fact, be harder than those from a standing position.

5. *Standing* (front and side):
   - Standing with step
   - Single leg

In addition to developing rotary power, the same progression of positions can be used for overhead throws for javelin throwers. Overhead throws should be done with two-to-three kilo balls. Care must be taken when providing stress to the rotator cuff.

Total-Body Power

As was mentioned in the introduction, the medicine ball is also a great tool for total-body power. This factor is particularly useful for athletes who are unfamiliar with Olympic lifts or have injuries that prevent them from performing exercises like cleans or snatches. In addition, total-body throws allow coaches uncomfortable with teaching the Olympic lifts to get hip- and leg-power work in a resisted situation.

Among the suggested total-body throws are throws from a squat position forward, a scoop-type throw from a squat position, and throws from the lunge position.

It is important that athletes do not attempt to catch a medicine ball thrown by a partner. Catching heavy medicine balls can be dangerous to both the shoulders and the fingers of the athlete.

Medicine ball throws should be treated like any other strength-and-power exercise.

Medicine ball throws should be treated like any other strength-and-power exercise. Doing 20-30 throws (two-to-three sets of 10) of each type twice per week is suggested. For rotational throws, the aforementioned progression is recommended. As the athlete moves from tall kneeling, to half-kneeling, and eventually to standing, the link between the hips and the hands will show rapid improvement. Throwers should perform rotational throws a minimum of two days and a maximum of three days per week. Keep volumes low-to-moderate and tell your athletes to throw the ball like they want to break it. For throwers, the medicine ball may be the most underrated tool to develop rotational power.

8

Six Little Secrets Every Thrower Should Know

By Jeff Chakouian

Strength and conditioning are crucial for any athlete's success. Strength training separates the average athlete from the above-average athlete and transforms great athletes into superb athletes. To be a high-level athlete, you must have strength, agility, speed, flexibility, and coordination. A solid strength and conditioning regimen increases all of these areas. Almost all strength coaches in the United States believe that their philosophies on training reign paramount. All of the coaches I have been involved with have their own philosophies and work for their respective sport. There are many different ways to train for the throwing events. The following are a few "secrets" that I have either picked up or devised along the way. Hopefully, you can use them to help your athletes.

☐ *Rest*. Recovery and regeneration are topics that are always mentioned but rarely understood. "Get your rest" is not good enough. Eight hours of sleep are recommended for the general population, but the majority of Americans are sleep deprived. As a serious athlete, you need a minimum of eight hours of sleep every night, and you should try to get more than eight hours. If you do not believe me, I urge you to take my sleeping challenge. Sleep one-to-two hours a night more than usual for one week. After this week, record how you feel. Seven-to-10 hours of sleep a night will make you feel more energized, less sore after a workout, and decrease your chances of getting sick. I took the challenge, and I feel like a totally different person, by just increasing my sleep by one and a half hours each night.

☐ *Jump rope*. Almost all throwers detest the idea of running. Coaches, nonetheless, have athletes run a warm-up lap at a lethargic pace. The jump rope concept can be dated back to the Middle Ages. There is a valid reason why jumping rope has survived so many years. Put simply, jumping rope works. A jump-rope session can be as simple as jumping over the rope

> Strength training separates the average athlete from the above-average athlete and transforms great athletes into superb athletes.

100 times for a warm-up activity, or devising a complete cardiovascular workout in 10-to-15 minutes. When jumping rope becomes comfortable, you can spice it up. Time the seconds it takes to get 50 jumps. Take a 30-second breather and repeat. A thrower will feel the effect after only a few minutes. Jumping rope can serve as a great warm-up activity, plyometric activity, and cardiovascular activity. Plus, you don't have to run.

Stretching is a key component of total athleticism.

☐ *Flexibility.* Stretching is a key component of total athleticism. There are two basic techniques to build flexibility. Static stretching involves the traditional "hold it for a count of 10" exercise, an activity which should be done before and after your workout. Ballistic stretching is the other primary type of stretching. Although, this particular technique has developed a relatively bad reputation, it can be beneficial if done properly. Stretching ballistic is a wonderful way to warm up, especially before a throwing session. Ballistic stretching should be done smoothly, not erratically. If you adhere to the proper technique for performing both types of stretch, you will truly benefit from both static and ballistic stretching.

☐ *Grip strength.* Throwing an implement requires solid grip strength. Grip strength is a measurement of the collective strength in an individual's hand, wrist, and forearm. These exercises should be completed four-to-five times a week. I am willing to bet wherever you work out, there is often a piece of wood with an iron plate hanging from it in the corner. Well, use it. Holding the wood at arms length and then turning the wood until the cord is totally wound up (thereby bringing the plate to the wood) is a great exercise for building forearm and wrist strength. Another one of my favorite grip-strength exercises is the raw rice or sand grind. This exercise involves placing uncooked rice or sand in a box and then grinding it with your hands. Knead the rice or sand like you are making pizza dough. Increase the speed and angles as you grind the rice. You will feel it after a half minute. This exercise can be very helpful, especially if you clean with straps, because when you clean with straps you lose a lot of hand strength. These two exercises can help increase your grip strength by as much as 10-fold.

☐ *Rhythm.* Throwers must have rhythm to compete at a high level. Repeat the rhythm of the throw in your head. If you are having trouble developing a rhythm, watch some film of world-class athletes and pay attention to their feet hitting the ground. It always helps to clap out the steps of the javelin approach. This applies to all the throwing events. When your feet hit the ground, there should be a clap in your head. Once you have the claps in your head, you can begin to feel the throwing rhythm. At some point, you may have to slow down in the back of the ring to establish a proper throw rhythm.

☐ *Hypertrophy.* Hypertrophy is a type of training used by many professional sporting teams. Many NFL teams have adopted hypertrophy philosophies, and most NBA teams use strictly hypertrophy-training methods. Many strength coaches believe hypertrophy is the only method of training worthwhile. However, in my opinion, heavy sets of five reps are the best way to develop strength. Like every other thrower in the country, I believe it is crucial to establish power with heavy triples and doubles. Hypertrophy can have a place in a sound training regimen. "Burn-out" sets are very effective if completed toward the end of your workout. When you finish your work sets, go ahead and try a few burn-out sets. Remember to keep it simple. For example, after you are done with your heavy bench press, crank out two burn-out sets of push-ups. Another option is when you are done with cleans, go ahead and grind out a couple of burn-out lateral raise sets. If you do two sets of burn-outs, your overall muscle fatigue will increase dramatically. Hypertrophy sets are not only a good way to build strength, but can be done without placing added tension on your joints.

Although the aforementioned six little secrets to success involve relatively small portions of your training, they are essential aspects for building athleticism. Many articles focus on an athlete's lifting schedule, but resistance training is only one piece of the puzzle. Above all, a thrower must be a complete athlete. One of the best ways a thrower can become a more complete athlete is by paying attention to detail. In some circumstances, what separates a good thrower from your personal best is a little more hand strength. In other situations, a mediocre throw can be turned into an excellent throw by more trunk flexibility. After all, the throwing events are competitive activities where the gold and silver winners are often separated by centimeters. You never know, the aforementioned training tips might be the difference between a thrower watching the finals at a big-time meet or actually competing in it.

One of the best ways a thrower can become a more complete athlete is by paying attention to detail.

Gray Mortimore/Getty Images Sport

9

Belief Before Proof: Throwing Really is a Miracle

By Joe Donahue

"There are only two ways to live your life—one is as though nothing is a miracle, and the other is as though everything is a miracle."

— Albert Einstein

Believing before *doing* is of primary importance, not only generally, but also specifically. It does require, however, an effective understanding of biomechanics, learning by the coach and athlete, and the rapport necessary for both to learn these in principle. In performing motor and psychological exercises, it can be effective to tell athletes to train muscle groups for the events and to *tell* the groups *what* they must do. Do not take the chance that somehow various body parts automatically follow the "correct" technique, without occasional direct intervention and cues. Have your athletes imagine/think/visualize what the movements look and feel like in the muscles *before* they do the movements, as well as after. They do not need to understand this before they do it. Extra intellectual activity proximal to the throw can cause motor conflict. Many coaches have discovered this. Yogi Berra, the great Yankee baseball catcher, used this phenomenon to distract the hitters' performance by engaging them in conversation, and it worked. "Keep your eye on the ball" can have legitimate merit for other sports as well, and we should add, "stop thinking about it, while you throw."

Extra intellectual activity proximal to the throw can cause motor conflict.

You can hear the verbal commands in many sports, which are derivatives of larger motor movement. In gymnastics, the vaulter is sub-verbalizing to "stick the finish." The metaphor is representative of a complex motor task. You can *whack* the finish in the shot or tell your thighs to push *down harder* as you squat. One is a general metaphor cue, and the other is a specific cue to a body part.

Andy Lyons/Getty Images Sport

Believing before doing is of primary importance, not only
generally, but also specifically.

Most of us want to analyze almost everything we must do, but some or most of the things that will be done by us come before we understand it. Remember how it was when you first rode a bike? You wavered and fell, and the next time (without thinking), you let your body do the adjusting. Soon, you were doing it automatically. The idea that understanding and *knowing* intellectually comes before *doing* and *discovery* is a rather new phenomenon historically. We can *blame* it on rationalism. It is not an accident that the creative efforts of many of the most famous and productive artists, musicians, and scientists in history came at the dawn or before the advent of rational thought on their part. Blame it on Rene Descartes, who developed the following Laws of the Cartesian Method:

- Accept nothing as true, which is not clear and distinct;
- Analyze a problem into its parts and discuss it part by part;
- Arrange thoughts from simple to complex as the order of study; and
- Enumerations must be full and complete and nothing must be omitted.

Most of us want to analyze almost everything we must do, but some or most of the things that will be done by us come before we understand it.

Scientists attempt to prove what cannot happen, and when something happens that they cannot explain (but they can replicate it), they call it discovery.

If we waited for all these to occur in throwing and other creative acts, we would be back in the dark ages of sport. Scientists attempt to prove what cannot happen, and when something *happens* that they cannot explain (but that they can replicate), they call it discovery. They then analyze it to death to try to have its phenomena match what they already believe. A rare few (e.g., Albert Einstein, Isaac Newton, Johannes Kepler) accepted what they could not further explain, and "it" became a law. Just "do it" and check the results after a reasonable amount of trials, modify the performance, then do it again. Keep in mind that the "ahah" comes *after* you stub your toe… not before.

Good practices in personal life and beliefs protect you from harm. Use the Cartesian method to examine what you have done after you have done it and away from the field of play. Effective science and discovery lead to good practice efforts from observing what works before understanding. As long as we leave a little pinch of curiosity and wonder for what we do, the "new" discoveries will come. "Ahahs" have their own agenda, and we have ours. Let us leave little openings in our "agendas" for the "ahahs" to peek through.

10
Reasons for Technique Breakdown

By Joe Donahue

This is a brief article focusing on some of the reasons a thrower's technique "breaks down." This first step is to go back to where your technique was together or congruent, as they say in counseling. At that point, work forward again until the technique begins to break down. This point is where you will find the basis for undertaking your analysis. Keep in mind that it is not always the most apparent and obvious part that may be at the root of your problems with your technique. Your whole technique involves a myriad of parts—each of which works in conjunction with the other *parts*. The key is to identify the aspect of your technique that is causing you problems.

> Your whole technique involves a myriad of parts—each of which works in conjunction with the other parts.

If some parts are more advanced than others, the advancement may place too big a load on the weaker parts. The weaker part can be developed, but only at the rate and load that the whole system can handle. Without seeing what you are *doing*, it is almost impossible to help without prior coach-athlete understandings. If you have some concern over general areas of your technique, you should initially look at the speed of the movement, and then balance. Are you moving at the right speed to maintain your balance? Are you on balance throughout the movement?

Intensity of effort from throw-to-throw and practice-to-practice may also be a factor. Are you practicing too intensely for too many throws? Such an approach can lead to a breakdown in technique. If your technique deterioration continues, do you keep on throwing so as to reinforce the *bad* technique? Do you have a part of your body that is more advanced in strength than most other parts? If so, using the stronger body part may place undue stress on the other weaker parts of the body. And finally, are you fit for what you are attempting and is the technique you have chosen fit for you?

If you think of your technique as a chain, you need to systematically examine each link in the chain to determine why your technique has broken down.

Always remember that things happen for a reason. If you think of your technique as a chain, you need to systematically examine each link in the chain to determine why your technique has broken down. Unfortunately, the process may not always be as quantitative as you might like. The key is to keep an open mind and be as analytical as possible in your analysis. As Albert Einstein once stated, "Not everything that can be counted counts, and not everything that counts can be counted."

Brian Bahr/Getty Images Sport

11

The Coach as Teacher and Motivator

By Joe Donahue

After a few years of coaching at my university, I noticed that some of my athletes performed much better in practice than in competition. (I was both a strength and conditioning coach and a shot put, discus, hammer, and javelin coach). I noticed this manifestation both in the event preparation and the conditioning phases as well. I studied this situation at length, trying different methods to make the competition the "real" event and not the prep. What I concluded was that a combination of two major factors—lack of confidence and pleasure/excitement—had combined to displace and redirect the purpose of the training.

What was practice and training had become pleasurable and confident. The "real" event had become unsure and reluctant. It was as if a schizoid atmosphere had embraced the athlete. I watched the body/eye cues of my athletes more closely and compared the two disparate venues. Given my limited observations, I began to prepare a new way to train them, employing several devices that I found helpful.

When my athletes did their supportive training, they would, at specific times, as the conditioning exercise came closest to their "real" event, visualize the event as they did the training. For example, a shot putter who *puts* a heavy metal ball would imagine actually throwing the shot, while pushing a barbell or performing a medicine ball exercise. I would often ask them to exhibit similar sounds (e.g., a yell or loud groan), similar to what they would otherwise emit during the real event. In the event training, such as throwing the shot put, I would cue them, at specific, lowered arousal times, no matter what they were doing, to match in specific terms what they did in their prep work.

This approach is a form of parallel chunking (a way of comparing a similar event under a different general category) and reframing, but the emphasis, cued by my own posture and voice, would emphasize that the goal was to *throw* far, which would occur anytime soon. My verbal and body cues always matched what I would use in the actual event practice. I would raise my arms and shout, "Far!"

Practice also has its own mind set and skill.

They were not allowed to throw their limit in practice and were required to stay within proscribed ranges, low-to-high, until a specific time period before a championship. This stipulation created a paradoxical effect that a long throw might accidentally "pop out" without effort to do so. It often built up a developing anxiety, which would be released in the "real" competition. I would adjust the range upwards, as their throws approached the higher range boundary in greater numbers. That release would bring a wave of excitement and pleasure at being successful, which—in turn—would reinforce the competition environment in practice learning.

Utilizing such a high-level competition and performance approach is a technique that involves a particular mind and skill set. Practice also has its own mind set and skill. The "range" of allowed performance widened their expectant focus and enabled them to accept lesser throws with the higher throws, thereby lowering their level of arousal. Once an achieved number of performances within the current range had been performed, the range was moved upward.

My rationale was that if I could get them to raise their actual performance at lower arousal levels, then the natural rise in stimulation that occurs in competition would cause them to perform substantially better, requiring only a slightly improved effort. Using numbers to categorize effort, as an example, 10 would refer to a maximum effort, while one would designate the lowest effort. Our training regime was designed to be a situation where a self-reported, long competition effort felt as if it were feeling like it involved a "six effort," when in performance it looked like an "eight" to me, the

Expect the training to work and let it happen.

observer/coach. In this instance, the athlete had successfully brought his arousal mechanisms under control and let the natural central nervous system reaction take place. As a coincidence to this competition goal, I found that the athlete's well-being, both mental and physical, affected their self-report in real ways. For example, they might report an "eight" effort when I observed a "five." This would alert me that something important was happening to that athlete at that critical point in time. It could be long hours of study, the onset of a cold, an emotional conflict, lack of sleep, etc.

I rarely, if ever, measured a practice throw, emphasizing the work done and the goals of the practice. I would constantly link an improvement, as noted, with a presupposition of a further effort in "real" competition. The links were always to a future competition, which was then linked with another. The following verbal presupposition for an athlete whose longest throw is 180 feet in the hammer (about 54 meters) illustrates my approach:

"Good, you're getting more in that range. That shows the jump will come anytime now, so you must be prepared for it. We'll probably move your range up a meter on Thursday (pacing forward).

"When you are at 200 feet, you will begin to notice that you're now "hanging" on the hammer in the back (he's never done this previously; it is a result and cannot be willed).

"This will keep you in better contact with the ball. You will love the feeling (expectation of result, and I demonstrate the position—future pacing) as the hammer throws itself.

"Your range will probably move up 10 feet in practice (beware, you are about to improve), so save your energy." (Throw what you have been doing with an easier effort and arousal level.)

Do *not* explain what is happening to the student/athlete; just let it happen. The student/athlete does not need to intellectualize the event...just do it. A former world record holder in the javelin, Al Cantello, once said to me, "Analysis leads to paralysis." Explanation takes away from the excitement of learning. In other words, an undue emphasis on identifying what or why something happens may in fact inhibit the actual performance of the task. The key is not to overthink the task at hand. Just do it. For the doer, the task is special—a feeling which you can link to future results.

Do not explain what is happening to the student/athlete; just let it happen.

I used these devices first as a coach, and then in the classroom, with my behaviorally handicapped students. They experienced similar results.

All my NLP (neuro linguistic psychology) training came after these events. The training confirmed what I observed. It worked because we both expected it to, and we *let* it happen.

12

When You Used to Play Football

By Joe Donahue

Question: Is it bad to see a decrease in the distance of my throw? I mean, I am maintaining the same strength and everything. I am trying to visualize my throw by taking it slow-to-fast but then I find myself trying to kill the shot with strength. What do you think I should do? This scenario involves my weekend throwing experience. Whenever you get a chance to reply, it doesn't matter when.

Answer: No, it's not "bad." Your body is in a down time for the shot and up time for football. At this time last year, you would have already played several football games and finished at least two months of pre-competition training, where the shot was pushed further back into your awareness. That is also after 11 years of the experience of getting ready for football. This set of circumstances allowed your body and psychological mechanisms to prepare for the contact of football. Many of your muscles and response systems are now being controlled by your "football" program in your head. Your "throws program" is still four months away from clicking in. That, however, is on your last year's time frame. As this year's experiences are embedded in your motor program, they will modify your "old" program and, in some cases, adopt a new profile for you to slip into. You must work at it, however, and pay attention to what your workouts are "giving" you.

The mind-body entity is a wonderful thing.

How was your "football program" in June? Not too sharp, I imagine. The mind-body entity is a wonderful thing. It accepts what you train it to "do" and prepares you ahead of time for the next trained phase. You can modify this "old" program by changing the method, the intensity, and the timing of your training regime. Visualization, for example, can be an effective "bridge" to these new motor requirements. For now, intensity and loading are important. Don't throw hard in real time or in your visualizations during this break-in phase. See yourself doing it effortlessly. In real time, if you throw, throw with ease and give up the distance for "feeling." One thing that helped a former thrower of mine who met Michael Carter (81 feet with the high school shot) is that he said he did "mirror throws" without the shot, moving very slowly through the circle and holding the finish position just for a moment, feeling every muscle into awareness.

You know you might have played that same game as a kid when you moved in "slow mo" in an activity, like a play fight or play football. It's fun, and it works. Michael Carter called it "mirroring," but it is the same thing as "slow mo." Do the slow mo backwards through the movement, starting at the finish and ending up at the start, and do it on the opposite side as well. If you throw right, do the left, and vice versa. That way, you can train your motor pathways and central nervous system with a light load, rather than an aggressive "hard" load, which is reserved for football right now. Soon, this "football time" will slip out of awareness. Visualize forward and backward as well, so that the movement is automatic. Remember this—there is no "right way" or "wrong way," just an effective way and a not so effective way, and the range of effectiveness depends on your body-mind abilities and what you believe at that time.

As a general rule, when the throwing deteriorates in marked fashion, you should modify the workout in a significant way or, if your throwing efforts are really ineffective, stop. There are no "bad" workouts, only workouts that send you a message about the way you are doing it, given your condition. When I say "condition," I mean the total body-mind thing. Some days, your body is ready but your mind is not; other days, it is the reverse. Remember when "it" is not working, you can modify the pace (i.e., speed and how often you throw and when) of the effort, the technique, the intensity (i.e., how hard you try), and the format (i.e., how you begin and end your workout).

When the workout goes well, you let "it" go the way "it" wants and no more. When "it" does not go well, "it" is telling you to do something in a different way.

When the throwing deteriorates in marked fashion, you should modify the workout in a significant way or, if your throwing efforts are really ineffective, stop.

Michael Steele/Getty Images Sport

13

Four Key Elements of Basic Hammer Throwing

By Bonnie Edmondson

For ease of discussion, a right-handed throw will be described. Reference points on the circle are as follows: back midpoint is zero degrees, and front midpoint is 180 degrees.

☐ *Posture*. The athlete must keep a solid athletic position (i.e., feet shoulder-width apart, knees flexed). The weight should be evenly balanced between both feet. Keep an erect torso—never bend at the waist. The body and ball work together as a system. There should be no segmentation between the upper and lower body. With the arms extended in front of the chest, the athlete establishes a triangle with the shoulders, chest, and arms. The head should stay within the triangle. The hips, knees, and feet should stay pointed toward the ball. The upper and lower body should work as one unit. Athletes should be aware of their posture and walk around confidently with their head up and their shoulders back. *Be confident and powerful*. This confidence will carry over to athletic performance.

> The athlete must "feel" the ball and visualize the throw, so the system works as one unit.

☐ *Rhythm*. The athlete must "feel" the ball and visualize the throw, so the system works as one unit. To establish a rhythm and orbit of the ball during the winds, the athlete should start working the ball early on the right side at approximately 270 degrees. This objective can be accomplished by the slight turn of the torso to the right and by extending the arms out to 270 degrees, while pushing the ball out and around. Each wind should be progressively faster, with the last wind being the speed of the first turn. Winds should be controlled, and a rhythm established. Sweep the ball out and around into entry. Set up the system and accelerate the ball through each turn. Left heel turn, right toe pivot, step under is the footwork sequence. To accomplish successive turns, simply push the ball past you, while pivoting your feet to 180 degrees and then step under with your right foot. The ball should turn the athlete.

Brian Bahr/Getty Images Sport

It is essential to keep a central axis of rotation, while maintaining good counter against the ball.

☐ *Balance*. It is essential to keep a central axis of rotation, while maintaining good counter against the ball. If the athlete sits back too much or gives into the ball (i.e., breaks at the waist) or bends left or right, balance and counter will be thrown off. Balance and counter directly affect the orbit of the ball. A strong core position is essential. An athlete must have sufficient core strength in order to maintain core position. Core strength is characterized by the individual's strength from her knees to her chest.

☐ *Ball speed*. Ball speed, at the moment of release, is the major determining factor in the distance of the throw. The athlete must keep her torso erect. If she deviates from the core position, the ball will decelerate. The system (ball and athlete) turn as one. Both feet must constantly be turning, with an emphasis on an active right foot. Strike the ball out and around to 180 degrees on each turn, while maintaining a strong counter against the ball. As the ball accelerates through each turn, the athlete must continue to counter the ball through the release. Think of the release as just another turn. *Be patient*. A common error is to "rip" at the hammer and rush through the release. As a result, the ball will be pulled out of its orbit and decelerate. The ball should create enough force to turn the athlete. This situation produces a very dynamic feeling. If the athlete tries to turn the ball, the result is a slower drag position, with the body ahead of the ball, thus diminishing ball speed. If the athlete is out of control, she may be starting off too quickly. Remember that the ball needs to be at maximum speed upon release.

Ball speed, at the moment of release, is the major determining factor in the distance of the throw.

This article complements a free instructional video "Basic Hammer Throwing—A Field Event for the New Millennium" that is available through USATF Women's Development. A copy of the video can be obtained by contacting Jeri Daniels-Elder at JDEHammer@aol.com or by calling (814) 234-3687.

14

A Beginner's Guide to Throwing the Weight

By Matt Ellis

Most weight coaches are either learning how to throw at the same time as their athlete, or they are hammer throwers trying to convert their old technique with a heavier ball.

The weight, no matter what age group you are in or what size you throw, is an event that has grown by leaps and bounds over the past few years. For example, many states now include it in high school, and the master's weight throw is currently being included in meets that never carried it before. With all of this interest, one problem that exists is that sound coaching for this event is very limited. Most weight coaches are either learning how to throw at the same time as their athlete, or they are hammer throwers trying to convert their old technique with a heavier ball. One of the primary goals of this article is to help clear up some of the confusion for beginner weight throwers and teach them the correct progressions to start throwing correctly.

First things first. What size ball do you use? In that regard, the following list details the weight of the ball that is utilized at various competitive, age- and gender-related levels:

High school boys	25 lb.	Men age 60-69	20 lb.
High school girls	20 lb.	Men age 70-79	16 lb.
Collegiate men	35 lb.	Men age 80 and up	12 lb.
Collegiate women	20 lb.	Women age 30-49	20 lb.
Men age 30-49	35 lb.	Women age 50-59	16 lb.
Men age 50-59	25 lb.	Women age 60 and up	12 lb.

(Please note: Youth weight throw is not recognized by the USATF as a sanctioned event. Some areas of the country do throw the weight in youth competitions. If you or one of your athletes is scheduled to throw in a youth meet, you will need to contact the meet director and check what size weight they will be using for the age group.)

Second, what size circle do you use? The circle used for the weight is the same size circle used for the hammer and the shot put. It is seven feet in diameter and does not have a toe board. The circle will either be made of cement for outdoor meets or wood for indoor meets. The outline of the circle can either be painted or recessed.

Third, what equipment will you need? To throw the weight properly, you will need to buy a good set of throwing shoes. The throwing shoes need to have a rounded bottom and can either be smooth or have a gritty texture. More advanced throwers will use the smooth-textured bottoms, because they can use them to generate speed. For a beginner thrower, however, the texture of the shoe sole really does not make a difference. You will also need a glove. There are many good gloves available from which to choose. If you are a right-handed thrower, you will need a glove that fits on your left hand. If you are a left-handed thrower, you need to get a glove that fits on the right hand. Gloves are made from all different types of material. Thick leather gloves will give you and your hand the most protection. On the other hand, such glove will not allow you to feel the handle all that well in your hand, and the leather will tend to bunch up against the handle. While thinner gloves offer little protection, they do enable the thrower to really feel the handle in his hand. Leather work gloves will also do the trick. Simply cut the fingers off and use a leather or Velcro® strap to fasten it onto the wrist. Of course, you will need a practice weight to throw. If you are just starting out, an outdoor iron weight will work well. If you are going to be practicing indoors, you will need to get your hands on a good indoor bag weight, so you do not damage the floor. Once these things are attained, you are now ready to throw.

The circle used for the weight is the same size circle used for the hammer and the shot put.

Matthew Stockman/Getty Images Sport

The release should feel like second nature to the athlete.

Next, how does the handle fit into your hand? If you are a right-handed thrower, the weight will be placed in your left hand (glove hand). Your right hand will then go below your left hand, so they are both cupped together inside of the triangle handle. Do not interlock your fingers. Start by getting a feel for the weight. Try swinging the weight between your legs and from side-to-side. At first, you may have to struggle to keep your balance, and your hand may start to hurt a little, depending on what type of glove you are using. After a while, you will become more comfortable holding on to the handle and the weight will not hurt as much. You will find that your glove will become worn where you like to place the weight. Once you are used to holding the implement and can keep your balance, you are then ready to try a few releases.

If you are a right-handed thrower, you will be releasing the hammer over your left side. Left-handed throwers will be releasing over their right side. All descriptions from this point forward will be for a right-handed thrower. If you are left handed, simply reverse the directions. Start the beginning of the throw with your knees bent at a comfortable depth and your back straight, facing the back of the circle. Start with the weight in your glove hand and begin swinging it back and forth. While building momentum, you will then cup your non-glove hand under your glove hand. Relax your arms and keep them as long as possible without rounding your back. Build momentum for the throw by taking a few side-to-side swings with the hammer. More advanced throwers will wind the weight around their heads similar to a hammer. Once you feel like there is enough momentum, pivot on your left heel and your right toe, explode by forcefully extending your legs, and release the hammer in an upward motion over your left side. When you finish, your feet will stay planted on the ground, and your body should turn and be facing the direction of the throw. Make sure that you fully extend your entire body to really put everything behind the throw.

More advanced throwers will wind the weight around their heads similar to a hammer.

Beginner weight throwers will tend to want to go right into the entire throw with different types of turns and technique drills. However, every weight thrower (particularly beginner weight throwers) should remember that the finish of any throwing event is the most important step. Make sure to get comfortable with your balance, with the feel of the weight in your hand, and with the full release. The release should feel like second nature to you. Once this factor is accomplished, you can then start to learn how to turn in the circle and release at the end.

15

General Physical Preparedness (GPP) for the Throws

By Matt Ellis

Through my journeys in the sport of track and field, both as a thrower and as a coach, one oddity has always made me stop and ask the question "Why?" And that oddity is why do throws coaches make their athletes, male or female, run long distances if they come into the season out of shape? I remember attending a clinic in Massachusetts where one coach blurted out, "If one of my boys comes into the season fat and out of shape, he's running miles until he gets better." Does this make sense to anyone? Would a cross-country coach make one of his athletes run 100-meter sprint repeats every day, or would a sprint coach make his athletes run six miles a day every day for practice? No! In any sport, especially track and field, you must train your athletes for what they will be doing. The issue is, how should this goal be accomplished for throwers?

GPP (general physical preparedness) has taken off in certain powerlifting circles and in other strength-related sports like the Highland Games, football, and wrestling. The purpose behind GPP is to still get in cardiovascular shape, but to do so in a way that incorporates general physical strength and speed. Also, it is fun. Running laps is dull and boring. With this form of training, you can make it fun by running two people against each other or making a competitive contest out of the activity. Another great aspect of GPP is that the equipment required is minimal, and pretty inexpensive, and can be kept in the storage shed with the shots, discs, hammers, and javelins. Furthermore, the coach can watch the athletes do the work. No more sending them off on their own. Among the different activities that can be incorporated into GPP training are the following:

The purpose behind GPP is to still get in cardiovascular shape, but to do so in a way that incorporates general physical strength and speed.

Sled dragging offers many benefits for throwers.

☐ *Heavy sled dragging.* Sled dragging offers many benefits for throwers. In fact, a number of your throwers may already engage in this activity if they play other sports. Sled dragging can get their heart rate up, provide a cardiovascular workout, and help improve both their leg drive through the circle and their total body strength. Have your throwers line up in two groups and race each other over a 50-to-60 yard course. While sleds can get pretty expensive, alternatives to such sleds exist, like tires, loading pallets, and homemade alternatives. In addition, a number of websites are available that explain how to build a good, cheap sled. Try varying the difficulty of sled dragging by having your athletes drag it up an incline or by adding weight to the sleds as they run.

☐ *Car/truck pushing.* This activity is not just for when your vehicle breaks down. Along the same lines as sled dragging, car or truck pushing can really provide a great total-body strength and cardio workout for your throwers. Don't want to use your car or truck in this activity? Undoubtedly, one of your upperclassmen would be happy to provide their car to help your underclassmen have a tough time. Want to make it more difficult? How about pushing the car up a slight incline or applying the brakes little by little. If you have hammer or weight throwers, try attaching ropes to the car and have them pull the car with a rowing-type motion. If you make it fun, they will do it and like it.

☐ *Heavy medicine ball/boulder carrying.* The activity is just like it sounds. Go to your local rock quarry or construction site and get some large, flat boulders. Have your athletes "bear hug" the rocks and walk with them a great distance. This activity can really test their endurance and give their abs, lower back, legs, and shoulders an incredible workout. Try making them walk in the long jump/triple jump pits or on the beach. Have them squat with the rocks every 40 feet or so. Really use your imagination and think of how to make the movements more functional for their specific events.

☐ *Farmers' walks.* As a thrower, the most overlooked and, in my opinion, most important type of strength is grip strength. Fingers, wrists, forearms, and hands get punished every day time-after-time and are really never trained. The farmers' walk will really help to improve the grip and hand strength of your throwers. You have a variety of implements that you can use to do this movement, for example, buckets filled with sand, weight plates that have built-in handles, hard suitcases filled with cement or rocks, boulders with chains and handles around them…anything. Just make sure your athletes grab one in each hand and get walking. This movement is also great for their endurance, and you can make the activity more enjoyable by adding a competitive element to it, for example, by rewarding the person who walks the longest.

The basis for my belief in the value of GPP training is my perception that the strongest people who ever lived were born back in the early 1900s. They were farmers, lumberjacks, miners, and railroad workers. They were strong because of what they did for a living. Back then, there was no such thing as Hammer Strength® or Cybex® equipment. They worked with their hands. Technology was not as big as it is today, and convenience was only for the extremely wealthy. People have called this "functional strength" and "grandpa strength," but what it really shows me is that full-body movements create total-body strength, exactly like the kind needed to throw. Isolation movements are great for bodybuilders, but you don't get style points in the throws: all that matters is how far the ball goes.

The key point to remember is this: do not replace your athletes' workouts with just these movements. Use these movements as a supplement once or twice per week in the off-season and every few weeks of the actual meet season. When you stop to think about it, adding these movements makes total sense. When your athletes step into the circle, there will not be a bench. There will be no weights or a squat rack. It will be them and their implement. They will need to rely on their total-body strength and endurance, not how much they can bench press on a SMITH machine. By using your imagination and creating exercises like those described in this article, your athletes will build the strength endurance they need to compete at a higher level.

You don't get style points in the throws: all that matters is how far the ball goes.

Scott Barbour

You must train your athletes by what they will be doing.

16
Teaching the Javelin

By Jim Giroux

The javelin, like the other throwing events, has its peculiarities. At 800 and 600 grams, respectively, these men and women's implements are the lightest of the four throwing events. It is the only throwing event that takes place outside of a ring with a long run-up. Therefore, greater demand is placed on transitional movement skills as the throw moves from a straight-ahead run to crossover strides and finally to the throwing position. This article examines and explains the steps and drills necessary to achieve a throw from a full approach. Each section of the article features technical points which you can use to cue your throwers on while they're doing the drills.

The Grip

In most of the literature about the javelin, three grip styles are discussed: the Finnish (the middle finger and thumb are behind the cord), the Ford (the index and middle are on either side of the shaft), and the American (the index and thumb are behind the cord). Research has been done on which style promotes better rotation of the javelin in flight and which one takes advantage of the strongest fingers in the hand. All three styles have several commonalities. For example, all three styles require that the palm should be kept up from the crossover steps through the delivery. Furthermore, the javelin should rest across the palm in all three styles.

When a novice or experienced thrower picks a particular grip style, "feel" and how the thrower gets behind the throw are important factors. Some throwers like to have the bony portion of their finger or thumb joint directly behind the grip cord. This technique gives them a solid surface to pull and push against when delivering the javelin. Other throwers slightly modify this portion of the grip.

> When a novice or experienced thrower picks a particular grip style, "feel" and how the thrower gets behind the throw are important factors.

Learning the Standing Throw

By using other implements (e.g., medicine balls, knocken, or javelin balls), in addition to utilizing drills performed with a javelin, you will be able to teach the delivery mechanics for the javelin from the ground up. Using medicine balls is a good way for the athlete to learn how to use the entire body to deliver an implement. Movements like jumping involve extension at the ankle, knee, and hip. The drills with the medicine ball move from directly overhead throws to throws that involve blocking of one side. On all of the drills described in this section, a ball that weighs between four and seven pounds and bounces should be used. From one-to-three sets of six-to-10 repetitions each should be performed for each drill. During the discussion of how to do the drill, it should be assumed that the thrower is right handed.

☐ *Straight-up throws*. Begin with a medicine ball just below your chin. Squat quickly and jump up, delivering the ball as high as possible overhead.

☐ *Unders*. Begin with the ball overhead, quickly bend and put it between your knees, and deliver forward in an arching manner as far as possible.

☐ *Russian twist*. Start with the ball at belly-button height, with arms slightly bent. Begin by moving the ball to one side. There are two crucial teaching points involved in this exercise. First, you should cue turning of the backside or away foot, so that the toe faces the instep of the other foot. Second, the thrower's body weight should shift completely from one side to the other on each twist. Move continuously from right to left.

☐ *Side or hip throw*. Start by facing 90 degrees away from a wall or partner. Begin with the ball at belly-button height and swing it back behind the right hip, shifting your body weight to that side. Deliver the ball at hip level. Move in the same manner as the Russian twist, turning the right foot and shifting the body weight over the front leg. Repeat throw. Also, perform the drill from the non-throwing side.

☐ *Two-arm javelin throw with a medicine ball*. Begin in the same position as the side or hip throw. Instead of beginning the throw when the ball is behind the right hip, continue moving the ball back and away, so that the ball ends up stretched behind your head and all your weight is on your rear foot. Just as the throw is starting, you should be facing the direction of the throw and have your shoulders square to the wall or partner. Use the same cues as before to get your body weight over your left side on delivery.

Throwing medicine balls allows your athletes to learn how to summate forces to deliver an implement. The following sequence of drills utilizes a javelin:

☐ *Two-arm throws*. Pick one of the aforementioned grips and put the javelin in the same delivery position as the two-arm javelin throw, adding your left hand over the right. Either step into the throw or do it away from a stagger position, as described previously. Pick a target a few feet away and try to hit it. Work your way down the field, slightly increasing the distance of the target.

☐ *Downhill-target throws*. Use a slight decline. Start the javelin at eye level. Progress in the following manner: A) start with feet staggered; B) start with your left foot next to your right and move it to the delivery position; and C) start with your left foot behind your right foot and move it to the delivery position.

Throwing medicine balls allows your athletes to learn how to summate forces to deliver an implement.

☐ *Level-target throws.* Use the same progression as in the previous drill. Increase the target distance as you work your way down the field. This drill can also be done from the three-step position.

☐ *Standing throws.* Begin with your left foot behind your right foot and move it into the delivery position. Keep your left shoulder even with your right when blocking. Keep your hand up so that the javelin tip stays level. This step will enable you to "get under" or "behind the javelin." Move your left arm from a long position, with the palm out, to an elbow-to-rib position. Keep your right side moving (pushing and turning), while your left side is getting into position.

Learning 3- and 5-Step Throws

The 3- and 5-step throws begin in the same position, with the javelin withdrawn and the right foot in front of the left. When doing throws from these two distances, cue the athlete to keep his left arm up and slightly bent, with the palm facing out (thumb down). The chin should be near the left shoulder.

Previously, the cues for the delivery and blocking action in "standing throws" were discussed. This section focuses on the action of the crossover steps:

- The next to last step with the left foot (the one taken before the last right) is crucial to the final throwing position. It must be active and link the acceleration of the previous crossover steps. Cue this action by reminding the athletes to keep moving. They will want to "get ready" to throw and slow down.

- By cueing the use of this step will aid in getting the thrower's block leg (last left) down faster.

Running the crossover steps normally takes some time to master.

Running the crossover steps normally takes some time to master. It is an acquired skill to be able to accelerate, while running in a side-on position. Fortunately, performing certain drills can help improve the ability of an athlete to run in this position, for example, the following lateral 20M movement drills. The athlete should do 2-4 repetitions of 2-6 drills with a jog return.

☐ Side shuffle with no arms; small amplitude side shuffle with no arms (vertical emphasis); side shuffle with no arms (horizontal emphasis); repeat above with arms, sweeping circles, carioca, small amplitude, work hip turn carioca, lateral emphasis; tapioca, lateral emphasis and high-knee action with back leg; crossovers without carry action, each side; and crossovers with carry action, each side.

The athlete should finish with eight-to-10M run, crossover every five steps; etc. The drills can be modified in several ways, including:

- Do some drills with the javelin
- Do eight-to-10 run, crossover with the javelin
- Do the drills up a slight hill

Learning the Approach Full Throw

The first part of learning the approach is getting the javelin withdrawn. This movement is completed in two strides. The completion of the withdrawal is the beginning of the 5-step position previously discussed. The smoother this portion of the throw can be, the less loss of momentum will result. The following action should be practiced walking, then jogging, and finally from a run:

The first part of learning the approach is getting the javelin withdrawn.

- Start with the javelin in the overhead-carry position (i.e., over the shoulder, flat, or nose slightly down), step first with your left foot, then your right foot (begin the withdrawal), and then with your left foot (the javelin is withdrawn). Check the position of the javelin and left arm and then repeat.

- Once this scenario has been practiced while walking, jogging, and finally running, begin to use it in connection with 5-step approaches. This undertaking will serve as a link between those throws and full approaches—first from a walk, then a jog, and finally a run. Once the javelin is withdrawn (i.e., the beginning of the 5-step throw), the 5-step portion can be walked, jogged, or run. You can throw from this drill or just run through. Adding the remaining steps required

Getty Images/Getty Images Sport

The javelin is the only throwing event that takes place outside of a ring with a long run-up.

to have a full approach is relatively easy. An 11-step approach is a good starting point. Some of the drills discussed in the 3- and 5-step section can help you transition from the run to the crossover portion of the approach.

- Start this approach with a left step (11 strides). Begin by walking the approach, counting the number of steps, and knowing on which one to begin the withdrawal. Practice this movement pattern without a javelin from a walk, a jog, and a run.

- Add the javelin and proceed in the same fashion with approaches walked, jogged, and run. No need exists to throw yet.

- Next, begin marking where the left foot (block leg) lands when running through the approach. When you have marked four-to-six approaches, note the distance, add a javelin length to it, and then measure the entire approach. This measurement can be done either by determining how many javelin lengths it involves or by using a measuring tape. Do this procedure on the same surface as you will normally throw from.

- Run the approaches either straight through as previously described or come to a stop around the toe board in a standing position.

The javelin throw's components should be practiced in progression so that there is a link in the learning pattern between the basic movement and the desired end result.

The javelin throw's components should be practiced in progression so that there is a link in the learning pattern between the basic movement and the desired end result. Because each portion of the throw is set up by the action of the previous movement, it is important to be consistent and practice perfectly so that the portions flow into each other.

17

The Discus Throw

By Jim Giroux

The Grip

The discus can be held with either a split grip (with even space between all fingers) or a grip where the index and middle finger are touching and even spacing exists between the rest of the fingers. Either way, the discus should rest on the last joints of the fingers (closest to the fingernails). Delivery should be against and from the index finger joint, with the discus spinning clockwise for a right-handed thrower. The thumb should rest on top of the discus. When the discus is delivered, it should leave the athlete's hand at shoulder height. Attempts to change the angle of release result in a throw that plows through the air. A good throw will appear flat and have an angle of release around 40 degrees.

A good throw will appear flat and have an angle of release around 40 degrees.

Grip Drills

☐ *Bowling*. Hold the discus as described previously, take a step forward with your left foot (for right-handers), bend at the waist, hips, and knees, and roll the discus forward. If done correctly, the discus should roll upright on its edge.

☐ *Standing releases*. Start holding the discus at arm's length, a little in front of your hip while standing. Move the arm upward and release the discus from the index finger, catch it in the same hand, and repeat. Once this step is mastered, athletes can swing the discus and release it higher, either catching or letting the discus land before repeating the drill.

The Stand (assume the description refers to a right-handed thrower for the remainder of the article)

During the stand, an athlete winds the discus into delivery position and delivers it. From the ground up, the stand requires the feet are wider than shoulder width, with an instep-to-toe relationship for the right and left feet. Line up with the shoulders square to the back of the circle (same as a full-throw start). The right foot should be in the center of the ring, closer to the front of the ring. The right toe should aim about 90 degrees away from the front of the ring. The left toe should aim at the right instep. The discus should be wound once and put over the athlete's right shoulder. Virtually all body weight should be on the right foot. Initiate action by turning both feet to get the body weight over the left leg. The feet should continue to turn until the right ankle is near the ground, and the discus is delivered. The left-arm action should start long and continue until the hand is aiming in the direction of the throw. At this point, bend the arm and bring the elbow to the left side of the body. Ultimately, this action should be well timed and occur together with the bracing of the entire left side (i.e., shoulder-to-foot). This technique is commonly referred to as blocking. The right side should then accelerate around the stopped left side, thereby transferring momentum to the discus.

Standing-Throw Variations/Drills

☐ *Stand*. See aforementioned description.

☐ *Figure-8 stand*. Start lined up as described in the previous drill but with the discus hanging near the right leg. Begin moving the discus in a figure-8 pattern over and under the shoulder. If done correctly, the pattern will be vertical. Master this drill without throwing before adding the throw. To add the throw, have the athlete finish winding the upper part of the pattern and deliver it as previously described.

☐ *Stepping stand*. Have the athlete start with both feet near the center of the ring, with the discus supported by the left hand above and away from the left shoulder. Simultaneously, wind the discus to the right shoulder and reach to the front of the ring with the left leg. Deliver the discus as described previously. Keep in mind that any of these drills can be conducted with cones, medicine balls, or other implements.

Step and Turn

The step and turn is the link between the front and the back of the ring.

As the article works its way to reviewing the factors involved in the full throw, the next aspect addressed is the step and turn. This element is the link between the front and the back of the ring. Begin with the right foot a little past the center of the ring, aiming between the center of the sector and the left-sector line. The left foot should be aiming in the same direction and behind the right foot, about shoulder-width apart. Start the throw by winding the discus back over the right shoulder and raising the left arm. As this action is being completed, begin turning the right foot and continue turning it until the discus has left the athlete's hand. The left leg should pass close to the right knee, land in the stand position, and turn to complete the throw. Once the left leg lands, you have performed a standing throw; in essence, this drill adds movement to the stand.

Step-and-Turn Variations/Drills

☐ *Step and turn*. See aforementioned description.

☐ *Continuous step and turn.* Hold the discus like a book, with the fingers wrapped around the edge. The discus should not be released on this drill. Assume the starting position previously described and stand on the line. Once the left foot has landed, immediately begin another step and turn back in the direction that you started. Continue for four-to-eight repetitions. When first teaching the drill, allow a brief pause on each left-foot touchdown.

☐ *Walking step and turn.* A discus is not needed for this drill. Walk normally and complete a step and turn every few steps, initiating the movement when your right foot is forward. You can stay upright while doing this drill.

South African

Begin this drill with the left foot aiming a little left of the center of the sector. The foot position should be where the full throw would start. The right foot should be behind the left foot, set up 90 degrees to the left foot, outside the rear of the ring. Most of the thrower's weight should be on the left leg. Wind the discus over the right shoulder and lift the left arm so that it is directly over the left leg. Run into the ring with the right foot, keeping the left arm up, while the chest runs into it. Think of pushing with the left foot, instead of reaching with the right foot to complete this action. By doing this, the left foot will land in front of the ring faster. Actively turn both feet when they land.

South African Variations/Drills

☐ *South African.* See aforementioned description.

☐ *Running South African.* Start with the discus slightly in front of the athlete, a little in front of the right hip. Jog a few steps, complete the South African drill, and throw the discus. Work up to a faster run to complete the drill.

☐ *Shuffle South African.* This drill can be done with or without a discus. Start with the feet lined up in the start position for the South African drill. Complete a South African drill, shuffle in the same direction once (your feet don't cross), and then complete another South African drill, followed by a shuffle. Continue in this pattern and complete three-to-five repetitions of this drill.

☐ *Continuous South African.* Complete three South Africans in a row. Start with a small, slow one and build on each repetition. Do the drill with or without a discus.

Full Throw

Begin in the back of the ring, with your feet wider than shoulder-width apart. Wind the discus over the right shoulder, keeping more weight on the left side than on the right. The athlete should be slightly bent at the waist, about the angle he will land in the center of the ring. The left armpit should be over the left knee at the start. Think of the left side (shoulder-to-foot) as being a door. It will need to turn together around the left foot until the arm points at the center of the ring. A couple of cues for properly completing this part of the throw are to stay bent and balanced going around the left side and to keep the right foot the same distance away from the left foot as it was at the start of the drill. Once the athlete has reached the South African position, the throw should continue as previously described in the South African.

Full Throw Variations/Drills

☐ *Full throw.* See aforementioned description.

☐ *Left-foot drills.* Do this series of drills with or without a discus. Begin with all of your body weight over your left foot. Keeping the right foot the same distance away from the left foot, touch the ground lightly with your right foot six-to-eight points around your left foot. The pattern is like drawing a circle around the left foot. Reduce the number of taps gradually until the athlete can complete a spin around the left foot without touching the ground. Try a complete left-foot drill just before performing a full throw, rewind the discus after completing the drill, and then throw a full throw.

☐ *Backwards full throw.* Do with or without discus. Complete a full throw, stop at the front, and reverse the action back to the start. This drill is a relatively advanced exercise.

☐ *Right-foot throw.* Start a full throw. Don't let the left leg land at the front of the ring. All of your weight should be over the right foot. Throw the discus from the right foot and continue bouncing on it to regain your balance.

Andy Lyons/Getty Images Sport

Attempts to change the angle of a discus' release results in a throw that plows through the air.

Five Days, No Meets

Monday

- Dynamic warm-up
- Pick a drill from each portion of the throw and perform it away from the ring.
- Throw the discus
- Weight training

Tuesday

- Dynamic warm-up
- Pick up to two drills from each portion; use cones or medicine balls if throwing.
- Medicine balls
- Circuits and/or sprints

Wednesday

- See Monday

Thursday

- See Tuesday

Friday

- See Monday

Five Days, Two Meets

Monday

- See previous Monday or Tuesday*

Tuesday

- Meet

Wednesday

- See previous Tuesday if you threw the discus on Monday, otherwise see Monday*

Thursday

- See previous Thursday*

Friday

- Meet

*The key on these days is to only throw two days in a row once (meet and practice) during the week. Try alternating the weeks; you may need to move the weight-training portion of your workout regimen around to complete two days each week.

Six Days, One Meet

Monday

- See previous Monday

Tuesday

- See previous Tuesday

Wednesday

- See previous Wednesday or recovery and weight training**

Thursday

- See previous Wednesday**

Friday

- Shake out

Saturday

- Meet

**Two days of throwing should be adequate at this point (Monday and either Wednesday or Thursday). You should do drills without throwing the discus on one of these days.

18

Basic Technique for Discus Throwing

By Mark Harsha

Goal #1: Discus Grip and Release

1. Holding the discus:

- Place the discus in your throwing hand.
- Spread the fingers out, with the index finger inline with the wrist.
- Place the first knuckles of the fingers over the disc.

2. Releasing the discus:

- When releasing the discus, have your palm down.
- Squeeze the discus out (bar of soap).
- Have the disc come off the index finger.
- Spin the discus in a clockwise direction (for a right-handed thrower).

> When releasing the discus, spin the discus in a clockwise direction (for a right-handed thrower).

3. Drills that can be used to help teach the grip and release (when performing these drills, a competitive aspect can be added):

☐ *Arm swings.* Use this drill to help teach the thrower about centrifugal force:

- Stand with your feet shoulder-width apart.
- Place the disc into your throwing hand.
- Swing the disc level with the shoulders, back and forth, catching it in your left hand.
- Feel the discus pushing out on the hand.

☐ *Discus bowling.* Use this drill to help teach proper discus release:

- Put the discus in your hand, with proper placement.

- Bowl the discus to your partner who is standing 15 feet away.

- Remember to squeeze the discus out, making sure the discus rolls off the index finger and does not wobble.

- Once you become proficient at 15 feet, you and your partner should move farther away from each other, or your should bowl at a target.

☐ *Throws for height.* Use this drill to help teach the proper release of the discus:

- Stand with your feet shoulder-width apart.

- Place the disc into the throwing hand.

- Swing the discus forward and back, next to your body, two times.

- After two swings, throw the discus straight up, using a proper release, remembering to squeeze the discus out. Make sure your throwing arm is straight.

☐ *Skip throws.* Use this drill to help teach the proper release of the discus:

- Stand with your feet shoulder-width apart, facing perpendicular to the throwing direction.

- Place the disc into the throwing hand.

- Swing the disc level with the shoulders, back and forth, catching it in your left hand.

- After two swings, throw the disc close to the ground, using a proper release, remembering to squeeze the disc out and keeping your palm flat.

Goal #2: Power Position

1. Body position in the power position:

In the power position, stand perpendicular to the throwing direction.

- Stand perpendicular to the throwing direction.

- Position your feet shoulder-width apart, with your left foot slightly behind your right foot.

- Be in an athletic position.

- Shift 80 percent of your weight onto your right leg.

- Twist your upper body completely opposite the throwing direction. This position from up above will look like an X.

- Keep your chest, knee, and toe in line.

- Extend your right arm out from the side of your body.

- Extend your left arm out from your body, with a right angle relationship to the right arm.

2. Throwing from the power position:

- Use cones when first teaching to throw from the power position, so the athlete does not have to worry about the discus falling out of his/her hands.

- Over-exaggerate the use of the legs in the throw, especially the hips.
- Keep in mind that the sequence of the throw should be legs – hips – legs – arm.
- Start the throw by turning the right hip to the front of the ring.
- Once the hips start moving, extend the legs upwards.
- Sweep the left arm out and around.
- Once the left arm reaches the front of the ring, bring it in tight to the body to form a block.
- Use the left side of your body to aid in accelerating the discus.
- Release the discus.

3. Drills used to teach throwing from the power position:

☐ *Heel turns with a partner.* Use this drill to help teach over-exaggerating the hips coming through before the shoulders. Surgical tubing could be employed to add resistance:

- Get into the power position without a discus.
- Have your partner place his hand near your right heel.
- Attempt to smack and drive through your partner's hand with your heel—focusing on the speed of your heel.

☐ *Cone throwing.* Use this drill to help teach any parts of the throw:

- Use cones so the athlete can concentrate on the throw and not the disc.
- Use cones for inside throwing.
- Use cones to produce a long pull.

☐ *1-2 drill.* Use this drill to help teach the thrower to keep the disc back on the hip:

- Get into the power position with the disc held in your right hand.
- On the command of "one," open your left arm to the throwing direction and turn your heel out.
- On the command of "two," complete the throw—release the disc five feet in front of the ring.

Goal #3: Middle of the Ring

1. Body position in the middle of the ring:

- Stand facing the throwing direction.
- Take a step with your right foot.
- Place 80 percent of your body weight on the right foot.
- Put your body in an athletic position in relation to your right leg.
- Align your body as follows: chest – right knee – right toe.

In the middle of the ring, put your body in an athletic position in relation to your right leg.

2. Throwing from the middle of the ring:

- Swing your right arm back where you can hit the right cheek of your buttocks.
- Point your left arm towards the throwing direction.
- Start the reverse 180 by pivoting counterclockwise on your right foot.
- Pick your left leg up off the ground and drive it to the front of the ring in a straight line, as your right foot rotates.
- Try to hit your right heel with your left foot, as it is being placed in the front of the ring (knee-to-knee).
- Complete the throw once you are in the power position.

3. Drills used to help teach the middle of the ring:

☐ *Reverse 180s.* Use this drill to teach pivoting at the center of the ring:

- Start with your right foot in the middle of the ring.
- Complete a reverse 180, concentrating on picking up your left foot and bringing both knees together (cue knee-to-knee).
- Don't forget that it is critical that your right foot does not stop turning.

☐ *Wheels.* Use this drill to help teach balance and continue turning of the right foot:

- Start with your right foot in the middle of the ring.
- Complete a reverse 180, concentrating on picking up your left foot and bringing both knees together (cue knee-to-knee).
- Keep in mind that it is critical that your right foot does not stop turning.
- Continue for five repetitions.

☐ *High knees.* Use this drill to help teach the transition from the back of the ring to the middle of the ring:

- Stand at the back of the ring facing the throwing direction.
- Bring your right thigh parallel to the ground.
- Dorsi flex your right foot.
- Point your left arm towards the throwing direction.
- Swing your right arm back where it will be able to hit your right buttocks cheek.
- Fall into the middle of the ring—do not step.
- Once the right foot makes contact, start the reverse 180.

Goal #4: The Drive Through the Center of the Ring

1. Drive or sprint across the ring:

- This phase of the throw is a transition from the back of the ring to the middle.
- The drive from the back of the ring comes from a push off from the left ankle and a strong high knee punch from the right leg.

The drive-through-the-center-of-the-ring phase of the throw is a transition from the back of the ring to the middle.

- Do not spend much time in the air.
- Once you've pushed off your left ankle, tuck your left leg close to your right leg.
- Drive down a straight line (backward seven).
- Push off your left ankle once you reach the three o'clock position.
- Do not step with your right leg; instead, let the ground come to your right leg.

2. Drills to help teach the drive across the ring:

☐ *South Africans*. Use this drill to help teach the sprint across the ring:

- Face the front of the ring.
- Place your left foot into the ring at the five o'clock position.
- Place your right foot outside the ring.
- Draw the discus back behind your hip, allowing your body to wind up.
- Drive off the left foot and make a wide arc, while leading with the right leg.
- Make sure you drive straight down the line.
- Once your right foot hits the center, continue to turn your foot, while you do a reverse pivot.
- Plant your left leg in the front of the ring.
- Get into a good power position to throw the discus.

☐ *Walking turns*. Use this drill to help the athlete become accustomed to turning:

- Perform this drill while walking around the track or walking to and from practice.
- Step with the left foot.
- Step with the right foot underneath the body.
- Reverse pivot on the right foot.
- Walk two steps and do another turn.

Goal #5: Back of the Ring

1. Body position in the back of the ring:

- Face opposite the back of the ring.
- Be in an athletic position.
- Raise your arms to your sides at shoulder level.
- Twist your arms and shoulders to the right, forming an X with the axis of your shoulders and hips.
- Shift 80 percent of your weight onto your left leg.

In the back of the ring, shift 80 percent of your weight onto your left leg.

2. Pivoting out of the back of the ring:

- Pivot the left foot (squash the bug) towards the three o'clock position.
- Pick up the right foot as soon as the left foot is pivoting.

- Work only the lower body; the upper body needs to stay back.
- Have your right foot take a wide and low path outside the circle.
- Once your left foot reaches the three o'clock position, drive and sprint to the center of the ring.
- As you are driving to the center, bring your right leg in towards the center of the ring (high knee locked).

3. Drills to help teach the pivot at the back of the ring:

☐ *180s back of the ring*. Use this drill to help teach balance in the back of the ring:

- Start in the back of the ring in a good athletic position, with your arms at shoulder level.
- Keep 80 percent of your weight on your left leg.
- Turn your arms and shoulders to the right to form an X with your shoulders and hips.
- Lock the arm back and turn 180 degrees on your left foot—slow and balanced.
- Keep your right foot away from your left foot.

☐ *Small steps 180 and throw (step and go)*. Use this drill to teach the back of the ring movement:

- Start in the back of the ring with a discus.
- Touch the ground with your right foot, while doing a 180 (small steps).
- Once you hit the three o'clock position, continue the throw.

When pivoting out of the back of the ring, work only the lower body; the upper body needs to stay back.

Tony Duffy/Getty Images Sport

19

Basic Technique for the Shot Put

By Mark Harsha

Goal #1: Shot Grip and Placement

1. Holding the shot:

- The shot should be held at the base of the fingers, not the palm.
- The fingers should be slightly spread apart, with the thumb for support.
- The hand should be bent back in the cocked position when holding the shot. It should look like you are carrying a pizza.

2. Neck placement:

- Raise the shot above your head.
- Lower the shot straight down until it is under your jaw.
- Push the shot into your neck.
- Lift your elbow parallel to the floor. Don't squeeze your elbow towards your back.
- Check to see that your thumb is pointing down towards your clavicle.
- Point your palm towards the throwing direction.

Goal #2: Delivery of the Shot

1. Delivery of the shot:

- Keep your eyes to the ceiling.
- Punch the shot away from the neck.
- Keep your elbow high at all times. Lowering the elbow can cause the shot to be thrown like a baseball and could result in an injury.

> The shot should be held at the base of the fingers, not the palm.

- Finish the punch with a flip of the wrist.
- Stop and lock the left side of your body to help form the block.
- Tuck your left arm close to the side of your body.

2. Drills used to teach the delivery:

Use the wrist-flips drill to help teach the proper release of the shot.

☐ *Wrist flips.* Use this drill to help teach the proper release of the shot:

- Stand facing the sector.
- Start with the shot above your head in your throwing hand.
- Flip the shot out of your hand.

☐ *Two-arm putts.* Use this drill for proper release of the shot:

- Stand facing the sector.
- Place the shot in both hands in the chest-pass position.
- Check that your hands are behind the shot and your thumbs are down.
- Push the shot out with both hands; make sure your elbows stay high.
- Flip your wrists at the end of the throw.
- Keep in mind that this throw can also be done with a medicine ball.

☐ *Arm strike.* Use this drill to help teach the arm delivery in the shot:

- Stand tall, facing the throwing direction.
- Place the shot against your neck.
- Sky your eyes to the ceiling and push the shot away from your neck, focusing on driving through the shot towards the throwing area.
- Flip your wrist at the end.

☐ *Bent knee.* Use this drill to help teach the arm delivery in the shot and show the importance of legs:

- Face the throwing direction with bent knees.
- Place the shot against your neck.
- Sky your eyes to the ceiling and push the shot away from your neck, focusing on driving through the shot towards the throwing area.
- While you are pushing the shot out, push up with your legs, extending the hips out.

Goal #3: Power Position

1. Body position in the power position:

- Stand perpendicular to the throwing direction.
- Position your feet shoulder-width apart or a little wider, with your left foot slightly behind your right foot (toe-heel relationship).

- Place your right foot perpendicular to the throwing direction.
- Be in an athletic position.
- Shift 80 percent of your weight onto your right leg.
- Twist your upper body completely opposite the throwing direction. This position from up above will look like an X.
- Align your chest, knee, and toe with each other.
- Place the shot into your neck.
- Extend your left arm out from your body, with a right-angle relationship to your right elbow.

2. Throwing from the power position:

- Over-exaggerate the use of your legs in the throw, especially your hips.
- Adhere to the following sequence for the throw: legs – hips – back – arm.
- Push the weight from the right leg to the left leg in an upward direction.
- When driving up with your legs, turn your right heel (hips) out.
- Keep in mind that a stretch reflex reaction will occur between your upper body and lower body.
- Start your upper body coming around.
- As your upper body comes around, sweep your left arm around and then bring it tight to your body.
- Stop the left side of your body to aid in accelerating the shot.
- Deliver the shot as previously discussed.

Over-exaggerate the use of your legs in the throw, especially your hips.

3. Drills used to help teach throwing from the power position:

☐ *Twists*. Use this drill to warm-up and to help emphasize the importance of the legs:
- Face the sector, with your toes pointed straight.
- Place the shot against your neck.
- Bend your knees.
- Twist your body to the right and down.
- Extend your legs and hips, and then throw, as detailed in the bent-knee drill.

☐ *1-2 Drill*. Use this drill to help teach the need to keep the shot back on the hip:
- Get into the power position with the shot against your neck.
- On the command of "one," open your left arm to the throwing direction and turn your heel out. Check to see if the shot has stayed in place at the back of the ring.
- On the command of "two," complete the throw—slingshot effect.

Goal #4: Glide Position

1. Body position in the glide:

> When gliding into the power position, push and then pull your right leg underneath you; it should look like the last part of your body leaving the circle is your right heel.

- Stand at the back of the ring, facing away from the throwing direction.
- Place the shot against your neck.
- Put your body in an athletic position, facing away from the sector.
- Extend your left arm out—relaxed.
- Extend your left leg back towards the toe board.
- Most of your body weight should be on your right leg.

2. Gliding into the power position:

- Tap your left leg for balance.
- Draw up your left knee even with your right knee; remember to keep your left leg straight.
- Do not allow your left leg to curl behind your right leg.
- Allow your hips to start to fall.
- Violently extend your left leg towards the toe board; do not lift up with your back.
- Push and then pull your right leg underneath you; it should look like the last part of your body leaving the circle is your right heel.

In the glide position, most of the thrower's weight should be on the right leg.

Matthew Stockman/Getty Images Sport

3. Drills used to help teach the glide:

☐ *Hip fall*. Use this drill to help teach the hip-fall action in the glide:

- Start in an athletic position, with your right hand up against your neck and your left hand extended out in front.

- Let your hips fall past your heels.

- Once your hips go past your heels, pull your legs back underneath you.

☐ *A-drill*. Use this drill to help teach the left-leg drive:

- Start in the glide position.

- Drive your left leg towards the toe board, close to the ground.

- Straighten your right leg to a point where the only thing touching the ground is your heel.

- Keep in mind that the finished position with your legs should be an upside down Y.

☐ *Step under*. Use this drill to help teach the glide:

- Initially, perform an A-drill.

- On command, pull your right leg underneath your body, turning your right foot at the same time.

☐ *Step backs*. Use this drill to help teach traveling across the ring:

- Start in a glide position.

- Take one step back with your right leg to the middle of the ring.

- Then take another step back with your left leg towards the toe board.

- Make sure your shoulders do not come around.

- Be ready to put the shot.

Use the A-drill drill to help teach the left-leg drive.

20

Weight Throwing: Correcting Technical Flaws

By Larry W. Judge, Ph.D.

Introduction

The weight throw is one of the most exciting and artistic events of indoor track, yet it's a relatively obscure event. It is left out of most international indoor meets and used mostly in training by European hammer throwers. The weight is only officially thrown in Rhode Island high schools. Club athletes throw in Washington and Georgia.

Many coaches and young throwers have limited exposure to the event because little information on the event is available. To some, the weight has maintained an air of mystery over the years to a greater extent than even the hammer. This situation has caused some coaches to shy away from teaching and coaching the event. The collegiate coach must teach an aspiring weight thrower from scratch. This scenario forces coaches to play catch-up and get athletes ready to compete very quickly. Unfortunately, a crash course in weight throwing can lead to technical problems, because it can take years for an athlete to establish an efficient turning rhythm.

> To be successful, an athlete must be able to tell the difference between correct and faulty execution.

To be successful, an athlete must be able to tell the difference between correct and faulty execution. A flaw in a weight thrower's technical approach cannot be corrected until that athlete can clearly identify and understand the cause of the faulty execution. Technical correction is further enhanced by numerous executions of the ideal technical model. This ideal technical model must be formulated by the coach to fit each athlete's individual talents and anthropometric characteristics.

Problems Facing Weight Throwers

For many throwers, technique is often a small part of the challenge of weight throwing. One of the main problems is a lack of specific strength and a corresponding lack of ability to move. The weight usually feels heavy to most hammer throwers. An athlete who doesn't feel "strong" with the implement won't be able to succeed. The throws coach must devise a workout that will improve the athlete's level of physical conditioning and simultaneously incorporate a working technical model.

Many coaches get impatient when athletes can't perform the ideal technique, yet coaches may fail to realize the real cause of athletes' technical difficulties: a lack of sufficient strength. Difficulties may be overcome by overloading the system in the weight room, throwing with overweight and underweight implements, and performing assistance exercises with medicine balls and kettle bells. This overload will eventually enable the athlete to advance technically and perform more efficiently.

Unfortunately, efficient technique does not result from copying the technique of a current champion. A champion's form may be optimal for a person with the same physical attributes as the champion but far removed for a person less endowed physically or less well-trained. Accordingly, the coach must set the model for each athlete.

There are a variety of techniques used in the weight today. The coach must choose which technique best fits the athlete with whom he is working. In teaching technique to beginners, special attention should be paid to the development of the "right reflexes," as technique can only be mastered if muscle contractions and relaxations can be coordinated and synchronized to produce maximum total effort relative to weight throwing. What is required from the athlete is concentration on the right movements. If the wrong reflexes are formed in the athlete's motor pattern, they are difficult to rectify. During the initial stage, the athlete should not be "distance conscious." Rather, he should be conditioned to concentrate on developing the right movements in order to establish the right reflexes.

If the wrong reflexes are formed in the athlete's motor pattern, they are difficult to rectify.

After establishing an appropriate technique for each athlete and drilling the proper reflexes, coaches must detect and correct faults in the athlete's performance. The greatest difficulty in this regard is locating the causes of the observed faults. According to Bondarchuk (Russian Gold Medalist in the hammer and coach of world record holder Yuri Sedych), there are basically two kinds of individuals concerned with performance-related faults in athletes: commentators and evaluators. Commentators concentrate strictly on performance and point out mistakes. Evaluators find the cause of the mistake and figure out how to fix it. For example, a coach may see an athlete's low point shift to the left (effect), but to be of assistance to him, the coach must identify the reason for the shift (cause), which may be over-placing with the right foot or tightness in the arms and shoulders. The coach must devise a way to train the athlete's motor pattern to become faster by either improving the athlete's physical conditioning or making a technical adjustment. When making corrections, it's necessary to be positive. Telling an athlete he is "too slow" conjures up negative images in the athlete's mind—the athlete may be going as fast as he can.

In working with weight throwers, the coach attempts to teach very large people to move with the grace of a ballet dancer. Herein lies one of the keys to successful weight throwing: balance. To complicate matters, the balance required from the weight thrower is a rotational balance seldom learned in traditional sports. On the other hand, if the athlete's rotational balance is lacking, a clean set of turns is unachievable. Because of the sequential nature of the turns of the throw, balance problems in the start or first turn have to be avoided. Each part of the throw can have problems that may affect the next part of the throw, and therefore, the final product.

The Start

At the start of the weight throw, the winds often cause technical problems. Because of the mass and the length of the implement, athletes may have particular trouble controlling the implement in winds. Problems like lifting the shoulders, flexing the traps, and bending the trunk forward cause athletes to lose their balance when winding. Reaching too far back with the hands when passing the weight handle over the head also causes balance problems during the winds. Other problems to watch for are basic body position errors, including not staying opposite the ball, bending the knees during the hook-up and not countering the hips in relation to the shoulders and the ball.

Establishing the proper low point in the wind is important in establishing balance in the first turn.

Establishing the proper low point in the wind is important in establishing balance in the first turn. Sometimes, athletes wind and keep the low point too far to the right. This situation can cause the athlete to drag the weight or to stand up, thus losing power and radius. Conversely, the low point of the weight's swing can be too far to the left, which results in a lack of power in the impulse phase and fouls as the weight hooks at release.

The athlete may not emphasize the forward and upward part of the swing. The winds are a rehearsal for the turns, and an overly short impulse on the winds is likely to lead to short drive phases in the turns. Keeping the arms long and relaxed is a challenge with a heavy implement. The range established in the pendulum and the winds must match that of the throw. Not raising the left heel when turning the trunk to "meet" the weight may also lead to balance problems.

Getting the ball moving in the start differs from athlete to athlete. Athletes can use a variety of techniques to get the ball moving prior to starting into the winds. The option of eliminating the wind altogether and beginning with the pitch start also exists.

Because of the mass of the implement, many athletes have trouble starting the throw. Athletes sometimes shift their weight to the left leg too quickly following the second wind. Such a circumstance can cause the athlete to overplace on the first turn, leading to an unloaded right foot and a choppy transition into the second turn. An off-balance start takes energy away from the turns and leads to weak positions. Poor balance in the entry causes the athlete to use the turns to resume a good throwing position, rather than using them to accelerate the weight. Sitting back opposite the ball is helpful. Controlling the height of the ball and keeping the eyes level aid in balance.

When winding, the athlete must block the right leg at the back of the circle in a good solid squat position with the torso erect; the blocked right side improves the ability to counter the weight. Since a poor start can create problems in the first turn, the coach must make sure the start is controlled. The athlete should stay opposite the ball during all preliminary movement and hook up with it at zero degrees. The hook-up sets up the balance for the whole throw. The thrower must establish a firm center by dropping the hips and firming up the midsection. It's also important that the athlete is balanced and effectively uses the right side in the entry. The right side must be established as the engine.

The Turn

The transition to the first turn is one of the most difficult elements of the weight throw. It sets up the whole throw, wherein the body becomes a rotating axis for the weight. Incorrect execution of this phase reduces the effectiveness of the turns and unbalances the throwing rhythm.

The key to the first turn is to keep the head in line with the whole "weight system." The feet, knees, hips, torso, arms, and head all must move in sync. A common fault in the entry is starting the left leg before the right. The athlete then tightens and loses radius, leading to an off-balance entry. Another common turning fault occurs when the right leg sweeps around the left in a wide arc. This situation causes the thrower to drag the ball, break the system, and catch the weight with a wide base. The athlete must think of closing down the knees and keeping the right knee behind the left. If the first turn is properly executed, the thrower should catch the ball at approximately 225 degrees with the torso in line with the ball and the head erect. The right foot should be placed on its ball, with the hips slightly ahead of the shoulders.

The key to the first turn is to keep the head in line with the whole "weight system."

Improved awareness of weight head speed leads to better rhythm. The thrower must look slightly to the right during the drive phase. When the athlete's head is allowed to move ahead of the ball, the athlete is unable to sense the speed of the weight head. Keeping the head still allows the athlete to use his vision to sense weight speed. The athlete must think of waiting on the ball at the low point with the shoulders back and the majority of the body weight on the left heel.

Another common problem is turning the feet too late and too slowly, so the weight takes the lead. However, this isn't a problem if the thrower can overtake the ball in single support—that is, when the athlete steps over the left leg with the right foot and is balanced on one leg.

Athletes may also place insufficient weight on the right side. Placing too little body weight over the bent right leg during the foot placement prevents the right leg from executing the drive phase. On the other hand, too much weight on the right side causes the thrower to lose posture. The athlete senses this and becomes even more active with the left side—that is, moving the right leg too slowly and too far from the left turn (often referred to as the discus leg). This turning in place causes the lower body to rotate more slowly. The athlete then places the right foot behind the shoulder axis in both the vertical and rotational planes, leading to a late placement of the right leg.

An athlete turns in the same place if he bends the head and upper body too far forward. This positioning is called "drilling for oil." To remedy this situation, cue the position of the shoulders at the low point, and instruct the thrower to slide the shoulders back and lift the chin progressively during each turn. Having the athlete think of sitting back on the left heel and pushing the hips forward at the low point is also helpful.

When the orbit of the weight it too steep on the early turns, the thrower gets pulled off the ground and loses contact with the ring. Bending the arms on the turns causes the athlete to lose radius. Instead, the athlete must keep the weight in front of him. The coach can cue the athlete by telling him to feel the weight on both shoulders. Flat orbits through 90 degrees help the thrower feel the ball.

The beginning thrower may not turn the left foot to 180 degrees on the heel, causing him to veer to the left side of the circle. This movement is referred to as "drift." Turning too long on the left before picking up the right foot causes the athlete to overplace. It can cause the athlete to turn in the same place. Overplacing is also caused when the athlete doesn't finish the drive phase with the right side. The athlete must think of pushing the right knee and hands through 90 degrees until the right foot comes off the ground. The orbit, called a "loaded step," is relatively flat.

The Head

Inability to control the position of the head is the source of many technical problems.

Inability to control the position of the head is the source of many technical problems. Where the athlete's head goes, the body follows. A beginning thrower may drop the head to watch what the feet are doing in the turns. However, dropping the head causes the athlete to bend over, with too much weight on the right. You must instead teach the athlete to control the head position. Think of using blinders like a basketball player does when learning to dribble.

An athlete may mistakenly turn their head in the back of the ring during entry into the first turn. Turning the head prematurely causes the athlete to drag the weight, thus reducing radius and ball speed. When winding, the head should be up, the shoulders should be level, and the eyes should be focused outside the ring to the right. Looking to the right catches the weight early in front of the thrower, thereby increasing the duration of impulse on the weight in the swings and creating more balance. Keeping an eye on a spot one-to-two feet beyond the ball to the right on the catch is helpful. It keeps the athlete from leading with the head on the work phase and into the next turn. The ball must pass the point where the thrower is looking before beginning the turn.

In more advanced throwers, difficulties arise in the later turns. An athlete often has trouble keeping the head in line with the spine. This alignment is essential for high-speed throwing.

The Shoulders

An athlete must control the position of the shoulders throughout the throw to achieve success. The shoulders must counter the ball in the later turns. A common mistake is trying to counter the weight with the hips. This action involves a very advanced technique that elite throwers use in the early turns of a throw to gain radius. They get their shoulders back in the later turns. If not, ball speed is sacrificed. It's advisable to go ahead and counter the weight with the shoulder right away to ensure balance and control. A weight thrower should keep his shoulders level throughout the start to create balance prior to entry into the first turn. The shoulder axis must coincide with the weight's orbit or trajectory.

A common problem with the shoulders in an intermediate-to-advanced thrower is dropping the left shoulder in the single-support phase to facilitate a longer radius in the catch. This action causes the athlete to bend the trunk forward on the work phase. The athlete may then lose acceleration and "drill for oil." The shoulders must follow the same path as the steepening ball. If the right-handed thrower raises the left shoulder in the single-support phase, he bends the right arm. That, in turn, causes the thrower to lose radius.

The Release

Problems in the release are almost always the result of a technical problem in an earlier part of the throw. If the center of balance is too far to the right during the delivery, and the legs are overextended, the thrower gets no power from the legs. The delivery may then be too flat, and the thrower may use only his upper body in the delivery.

Problems in the release are almost always the result of a technical problem in an earlier part of the throw.

Countering is very important in the release. The back must be firm to prevent the thrower's torso from absorbing ballistic force from the legs. The arms must be kept long to keep angular velocity high.

After the delivery, a number of problems can occur. These include stopping the rotation instead of following through or stepping out of the front half of the circle instead of lifting the implement. These faults can be corrected by drilling the athlete in one- or two-turn throws.

Another common mistake is to watch the throw sail away. Watching the throw land is a sure way to foul. To achieve maximum radius, the athlete must look up at release to maintain control and stay in the ring. The cue is "eyes to the sky." The distance from the back of the head to the implement needs to be maximized. If it's a good throw, the athlete can regain control and still see it land.

Conclusion

Coaches must attack the athlete's main areas of weakness. Working on these common technical problems can solve many difficulties for the young thrower. Coaches must also be aggressive when analyzing technique. Doing many throws is important, but doing them correctly is the key. Observe the throw from different vantage points on the field. Use video to analyze the throw and to show the athlete what his technique looks like. Use videos of top-level throwers to show technical points to the athlete.

Many coaches attempt to correct the effect that they have detected and miss the underlying cause that produced it.

Many coaches attempt to correct the effect that they have detected and miss the underlying cause that produced it. This approach is analogous to a doctor treating only the symptoms of a disease. A throws coach must be equipped with knowledge of biomechanics to choose appropriate techniques and detect the root of faults in an athlete's execution. If an athlete has trouble turning the right leg, create drills to teach him how to feel the correct sensation. Be creative and devise your own drills or aids to help you teach the correct feel. Talk to another coach or a high-level thrower to find out what innovations they use in teaching or learning the throw.

Athletes and coaches, alike, are always seeking a magical formula for success. The only way to achieve success in the weight is by following a consistent training regimen that incorporates a system of overload, progressive resistance, and recovery.

Each athlete differs in natural talent and physical characteristics. Therefore, the coach must choose a model that best fits each athlete. The bottom line is: Select a model that's strong, snappy, and dynamic. Remember that there is no magic answer or workout for success in the throws, but there are ways to make the magic happen.

Gray Mortimore/Getty Images Sport

21

Neural Adaptations with Sport-Specific Resistance Training in Highly Skilled Athletes

By Larry W. Judge, Chad Moreau,* and Jeanmarie R. Burke**

Study Summary

The aim of this study was to assess the effects of variations in the volume and intensity of resistance training in highly skilled athletes on neural adaptive mechanisms: the maximality and pattern of neural drive. The maximality of muscle activation was measured using a high-resolution sample and hold amplifier to record interpolated twitches. The pattern of neural drive was measured by analyzing isometric torque-time curves and electromyographic (EMG) characteristics during the performance of rapid isometric contractions at maximal effort. The volume and intensity of training were varied at four weekly intervals to systematically emphasize the development of strength, power, and motor performance in 14 highly skilled track and field athletes (e.g., discus, hammer, javelin, shot put, and weight). Knee-extension strength increased significantly by 15 percent during steady maximal isometric contractions and by 24 percent during rapid isometric contractions at maximal effort after the 16-week program ($P < 0.05$). Increases in EMG amplitude and rate of EMG activation indicated that improvements to the pattern of neural drive occurred with sport-specific resistance training ($P < 0.05$). The maximality and pattern of neural drive did not change in the control group.

Keywords: human neuromuscular systems, isometric strength gains, neural drive.

Introduction

Neural adaptations after resistance training among initially untrained individuals include early activation, extra doublets, and increases in maximal discharge rates of single motor units (Kamen *et al.*, 1998; Van Cutsem *et al.*, 1998). In individuals with a prolonged background in strength training, the profile of neuromuscular adaptations to systematic variations in training load and intensity consists of concomitant changes to muscle strength and maximal levels of electromyographic (EMG) activity, with only minor changes to muscle size (Hakkinen *et al.*, 1987, 1988, 1991). These data tend to support the hypothesis that contributions of neural adaptations to periodic strength gains may be greater than hypertrophic adaptations in highly trained athletes (Hakkinen *et al.*, 1985a, 1987, 1988; Hakkinen, 1978; Hakkinen and Pakarinen, 1991); Hakkinen and Kallinen, 1994). It has also been hypothesized that neural adaptations induced by periodization of training may be essential for improving the technical aspects of athletic skill performance (Sale, 1988; Hakkinen, 1989; Moritani, 1993; Kramer *et al.*, 1998). Scientific evidence for this hypothesis is lacking, because systematic evaluations of sport-specific resistance-training programs in highly skilled athletes are limited.

The aim of this study was to assess the effects of variations in the volume and intensity of resistance training in highly skilled athletes on neural-adaptive mechanisms: the maximality and pattern of neural drive (Enoka, 1997). The maximality of muscle activation was measured using a high-resolution sample and hold amplifier to record interpolated twitches (Hales and Gandevia, 1988; Allen *et al.*, 1995). The pattern of neural drive was measured by analyzing isometric torque-time curves and EMG characteristics during the performance of rapid isometric maximal voluntary contractions (MVCs) (Hakkinen *et al.*, 1985a, b).

Methods

☐ *Participants and experimental design*

During a 16-week sport-specific resistance-training program, neuromuscular adaptations in the right quadriceps muscle of 14 collegiate field-event athletes (eight males, six females; height 1.82 ± 0.09 m; mean $\pm$ s) were assessed monthly between September (pre-training) and December. The events participated in included the discus, hammer, javelin, shot put, and weight. All procedures were approved by the local ethics committee. Eight college-aged individuals (five males, three females; height 1.72 ± 007 m) served as the control group. For the duration of the study, the control group was not allowed to participate in resistance training, but they were instructed to maintain their normal pattern of physical activity. The control group was tested in September and November. The physical characteristics of the participants are summarized in Table 1.

☐ *Training*

The athletes followed individual training schedules designed by the Olympic-level coaching staff. The coaching staff supervised all training sessions to substantiate strict adherence to the training schedules. All training schedules were divided into four phases: (1) strength-conditioning phase, weeks one to four; (2) strength-development phase, weeks five to eight; (3) strength-power phase, weeks nine to 12; and (4) peaking and maintenance phase, weeks 13 to 16. Laboratory assessments of neuromuscular performance were performed at the end of each training phase. The data collected after the strength-conditioning phase served as the pre-training baseline values in an attempt to control variations in the athletes' adherence to their off-season conditioning programs.

The goals of the sport-specific resistance-training program were to develop maximal strength and power of the major muscle groups of the upper and lower extremities and the trunk, as well as to improve strength, power, and techniques that are specific to throwing field implements (Judge, 1992). Exercises included the following: warm-up and flexibility drills, a general strength circuit consisting of many body-weight exercises, medicine ball and plyometric exercises, sprinting, classic power lifts, Olympic lifts, and throwing-sequence drills with overweight implements.

Progressive *heavy* resistance training was emphasized during the first two training phases when performing all exercises (Hakkinen, 1989). During the strength-conditioning phase, the athletes, on average, performed four sets of eight-to-10 repetitions at 60 percent of their one-repetition maximums for the various exercises. Training intensity increased to one-to-four sets of five repetitions at 85 percent of one-repetition maximums for the various exercises during the strength-development phase. In summary, the sport-specific resistance-training program progressed from initially high-volume, low-intensity protocols towards low-volume, high-intensity protocols over the first eight weeks.

During the strength-power phase, training intensity decreased slightly to one-to-four sets of eight repetitions at 80 percent of one-repetition maximums for the various exercises. Modifications to exercises included three-to-five sets of single repetitions of power lifts and Olympic lifts in which the weight was released at the end of the movement. Maximal single-repetition efforts during the medicine ball and plyometric exercises were also included. Progressive "explosive-type" resistance training was the goal of this phase when performing all exercises (Hakkinen, 1989).

As the athletes progressed to the peaking and maintenance phase, exercises were limited to three-to-five repetitions of the classic power lists and Olympic lifts at 80-to-90 percent of one-repetition maximums. The main emphasis in this phase was on improving neuromuscular coordination, as the athletes were training specifically to improve the technical aspects of the throwing motion to optimize athletic performance (Jones *et al.*, 1989).

□ *Apparatus*

The right-knee extensors were tested in a custom-made dynamometer (Edwards *et al.*, 1977; Koceja *et al.*, 1991). The participants sat on a straight-backed chair with their thighs supported by the seat, their pelvis secured by a seatbelt, their arms crossed over the chest, and their hips and knees flexed at 90 degrees. Quadriceps force was measured by strapping the lower leg to an aluminium plate (26.7 x 5.08 x 1.27 cm) that was instrumented with an electromechanical load cell (Interface, Scottsdale, AZ; liner to 3 kN). The aluminium plate-load cell device was positioned just proximal to the malleoli.

The torques developed during isometric knee extensions and twitch contractions were calculated from the forces sensed with the load cell and by measuring the distance, in meters, between the axis of the participant's knee and the load cell. The signal from the load cell was amplified and collected with an analog-to-digital (A/D) converter (Data Translation, Model 2801a, 1 kHz sampling rate) interfaced to a computer. Customized software was used for data acquisition and data analyses.

		Test session			
Variables	Group	1	2	3	4
Mass (kg)	Controls	70.0 ± 12.6	—	70.5 ± 12.7	—
	Athletes	96.8 ± 14.1	96.6 ± 13.7	96.6 ± 13.9	96.9 ± 13.8
Body composition (% fat)	Athletes	16.7 ± 5.70	16.2 ± 5.53	16.1 ± 5.14	15.8 ± 5.63
Overhead shot distance (m)	Athletes	14.3 ± 1.43	14.8 ± 1.65	15.2 ± 1.52	15.6 ± 1.52
Long jump distance (m)	Athletes	2.48 ± 0.29	2.55 ± 0.32	2.52 ± 0.28	2.58 ± 0.29
Vertical jump height (cm)	Athletes	9.17 ± 1.37	9.38 ± 1.57	9.67 ± 1.42	9.88 ± 1.30

Note: Performances by the athletes on the overhead shot, long jump, and vertical jump were obtained from the coaches' practice records.

Table 1. Characteristics of the participants (means ± s)

□ *Electrical stimulation*

Twitch contractions of the right knee extensors were evoked by percutaneous muscle stimulation. A pair of 8 x 12 cm pad electrodes treated with conducting gel was placed transversely over the right anterolateral thigh at the mid level. The mid-thigh level was determined as the equidistance between the inguinal crease and the base of the patella. The stimuli were square-wave voltage pulses of 2 ms duration delivered from an electrical stimulator (Teca Model M Stimulator, 0-300 volts output).

□ *Measurement of voluntary isometric strength*

At the onset of the protocol, three 100 percent MVC trials were recorded on a digital oscilloscope as "warm-up" contractions. Each of the three trials consisted of a 2 s increase to maximum knee-extension torque by isometrically contracting the right quadriceps muscle. Maximum torque was maintained for 2 s, and then the participant was instructed to relax. A fourth trial was included if the peak torques on the first three 100 percent MVC trials differed by more than five percent. The peak torque obtained from the "warm-up" MVC producing the maximal response was recorded.

□ *Measurement of resting muscle twitches*

Peak torque of a resting muscle twitch was evoked by delivering a single supramaximal stimulus to the relaxed quadriceps muscle. The use of a supramaximal stimulus insured that the same constant fraction of the whole muscle was electrically activated on each trial (Bigland-Ritchie et al., 1986). Three twitch contractions were collected with the A/D data-acquisition system. Twitch measurements were peak torque, contraction time (time to peak torque), and half-relaxation time. The measurements obtained from the twitch contraction evoking the maximal peak torque were used in the statistical analyses.

☐ *Measurement of voluntary activation of the quadriceps muscle during maximal isometric contractions*

The interpolated twitch technique of Hales and Gandevia (1988) was used to measure the extent of voluntary activation of the quadriceps muscle during a 100 percent MVC. The participants were instructed to increase leg-extensor torque gradually over 2 s to maximum and then, while holding this 100 percent MVC torque, a single supramaximal stimulus was delivered to the quadriceps muscle. The interpolated twitch method was repeated three times. There were approximately 60 s between maximal contractions. To encourage maximal efforts during each contraction, a target line was displayed on the oscilloscope that was 20 percent above the maximal peak torque of the "warm-up" MVC. The participants also received verbal encouragement (normal tone of voice) to reach the target line.

The load cell was interfaced to a differential gain amplifier with a sample and hold circuit (Hales and Gandevia, 1988). When triggered, the sample and hold circuit measured the ongoing MVC torque or bias voltage. The bias voltage was then subtracted from the subsequent load-cell signal to measure the interpolated twitch response at a gain of 20 and a resolution of 0.012 N · m. In practice, the resolution of the interpolated twitch amplitude is one percent of the amplitude of the resting muscle twitch, due to biological fluctuations in muscle torque production. The two output channels from the differential gain amplifier with a sample and hold circuit were collected with the A/D data acquisition system (1 kHz sampling rate per channel).

The dependent variables were peak torque of the voluntary muscle contraction and peak torque, contraction time, half-relaxation time of the interpolated twitch response. The level of voluntary activation was calculated as $(((a - b)/a) \times 100)$, where a is the resting twitch torque and b is the interpolated twitch torque. Dependent variables obtained from the voluntary muscle contraction producing the maximal peak torque response were used in the statistical analyses.

☐ *Torque-time curve analyses and EMG recordings of rapid isometric MVC responses*

The participants were instructed to reach maximum isometric torque as fast as possible, maintain maximum torque for 2 s, and then relax. The participants performed the task three times, with an inter-trial interval of 60 s. The EMG activity from the mid-belly of the right rectus femoris muscle was recorded with surface-recording electrodes (four mm in diameter; bipolar electrode configuration). The torque response and EMG activity were collected with the A/D data-acquisition system. The sampling rate was 1 kHz per channel. The position of the recording electrodes, with respect to the base of the patella, was recorded to ensure similar electrode placement for each test session.

The dependent variables from the torque-time curve analyses were peak torque, contraction time, and the average torque produced in 100 ms time periods from the onset of the torque production and overlapped by 50 ms (Hakkinen et al., 1985a). Contraction time was the interval between the onset of torque production and maximal torque production of the MVC response. Maximum integrated EMG (iEMG) and iEMG-time curve parameters were calculated from the EMG activity on each trial. The maximum iEMG value was calculated from the EMG activity on each trial. The maximum iEMG value was calculated as the sum of EMG activity during the contrction time and expressed for 1 s. In the iEMG-time analysis, the iEMG values (expressed for 1 s) were calculated for the same 100 ms time periods that were used in the torque-time analysis. These iEMG data points reflected the pattern of neural drive. The dependent variables obtained from the rapid isometric contraction producing the maximal peak torque response were used in the statistical analyses.

☐ *Statistical analysis*

A group by test session analysis of variance (ANOVA) was used to reveal neuromuscular adaptations in highly skilled athletes participating in a sport-specific resistance-training program. Because of the missing test sessions in the control group, a single-factor (test sessions) repeated-measures ANOVA was used to reveal the time course of the neuromuscular adaptations in the highly skilled athletes. These analyses of variance incorporated the Newman-Keuls *post-hoc* test to detect progressive neuromuscular adaptations and Dunnett's *post-hoc* test to detect changes with respect to pre-training values. Statistical significance was set at $P < 0.05$.

Results

☐ *Resting muscle twitch, muscle strength, and voluntary activation*

Twitch torque, MVC torque, and voluntary activation did not change between test sessions for the controls ($P < 0.05$). In the control group, the intra-class reliability coefficients for these dependent variables between test sessions were 0.67, 0.95, and 0.95, respectively. Twitch torque (35.2 ± 11.8 *vs.* 28.9 ± 8.96 N · m), contraction time (84.9 ± 9.99 *vs.* 83.6 ± 9.53 ms), and half-relaxation time (64.3 ± 12.5 *vs.* 59.4 ± 9.62 ms) of the resting muscle twitch were similar between the athletes and controls ($P > 0.05$). The contractile properties of the resting muscle twitch did not change with training in the athletes.

The MVC torque increased during the strength-training program as revealed by a significant test session main effect ($P < 0.05$; repeated-measures ANOVA) (Figure 1a). Compared with pre-training, the athletes showed a significant 10-percent increase in MVC torque at test session three and a subsequent 15-percent increase at test session four ($P < 0.05$; Dunnett's *post-hoc* test). Voluntary activation of the quadriceps muscle did not change during the training program ($P < 0.05$) (Figure 1b).

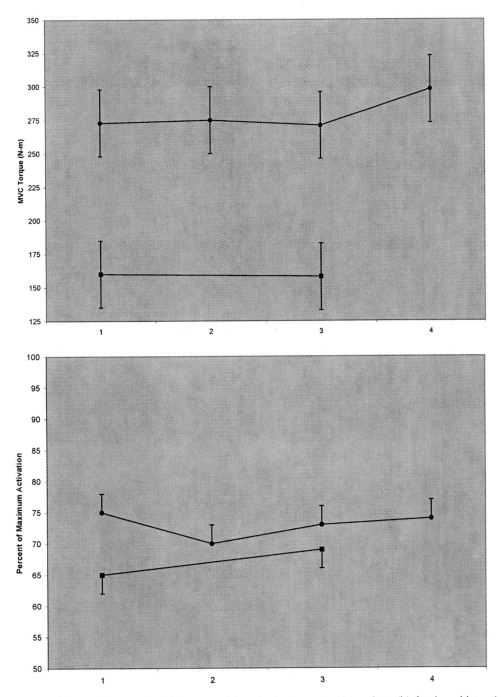

Figure 1. Changes in isometric MVC torques (a) and voluntary activation values (b) for the athletes ($n =$ 14) and the controls ($n = 8$) across test sessions. Error bars represent the standard errors of the means. ● athletes; ■ controls.

☐ *Torque-time curve analyses and EMG recordings of rapid isometric MVC responses*

Peak torque, maximal iEMG, and contraction time did not change between test sessions for the controls ($P < 0.05$). (Figure 2 and Table 2). In the controls, the intra-class reliability coefficients for these dependent variables between test sessions were 0.84, 0.64, and 0.87, respectively.

A significant group by test session interaction term was revealed for peak torque ($P < 0.05$) (Figure 2a). In the trained athletes, peak torque increased by 12 percent from test session one to test session two ($P < 0.05$). Increases in peak torque from pre-training values were also observed in test sessions three (19 percent) and four (24 percent; $P < 0.05$). Peak torque for the athletes was greater than for the controls at each test session ($P < 0.05$).

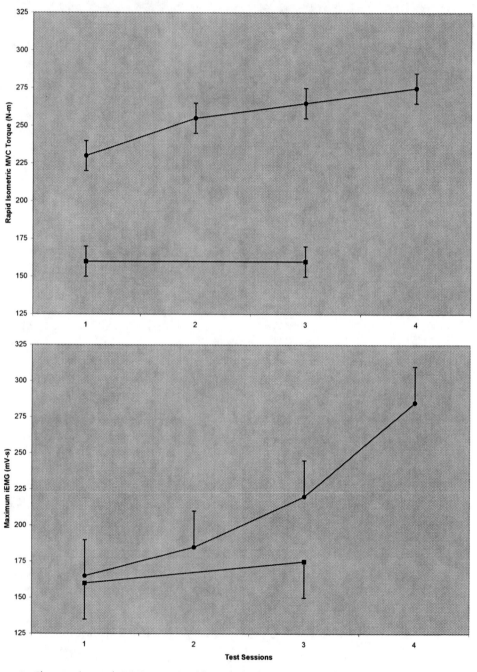

Figure 2. Changes in peak MVC torques (a) and maximum iENG values (b) during rapid isometric contractions at maximal effort for the athletes and the controls across test sessions. Error bars represent the standard errors of the means. ● athletes; ■ controls.

The analysis of the simple main effects of test sessions revealed that increases in maximum iEMG were significant for the athletes but not for the controls (Figure 2b). In the athletes, maximum iEMG increased by 71 percent from test session one to test session four ($P < 0.05$). Although maximum iEMG was similar in the two groups at test session one, maximum iEMG was significantly greater in the athletes than in the controls at test session four ($P < 0.05$). The relationship between increases in peak MVC torque and increases in iEMG among the athletes was $r = 0.63$.

Test session	Trained athletes	Controls
1	355.1 ± 225.5	316.4 ± 92.28
2	335.1 ± 138.1	
3	392.9 ± 219.7	326.6 ± 78.30
4	384.9 ± 139.4	

Table 2. Contraction times (ms) for the rapid isometric force development task across test sessions (means ± s).

Contraction times were similar in the two groups across the test sessions (Table 2). However, significant group by test session by time period interaction terms ($P < 0.05$) were revealed for averaged torques (Figure 3) and averaged iEMG values (Figure 4). Averaged torques and averaged iEMG values by time periods were similar for the two tests sessions in the controls ($P < 0.05$) (Figures 3b and 4b). The average amounts of torque produced by the athletes between 200 and 400 ms after the onset of the isometric contraction were significantly greater during test sessions two, three, and four ($P < 0.05$) (Figure 3a). In addition, the average amounts of iEMG generated by these athletes between 100 and 200 ms after the onset of the isometric contraction were significantly greater during test session four than during the other three test sessions ($P < 0.05$) (Figure 4a).

☐ *Evaluation of athletic performance*

Ten of the athletes participated in NCAA championship meets. Thirteen All-American honors and nine conference championships were earned by the athletes. One American record and one world record were set by the athletes. These results demonstrated that this pre-season training regimen induced the appropriate neuromuscular adaptations necessary for successful throwing performance.

In addition, performances of the overhead shot, long jump, and vertical jump improved from test session one to test session four by nine percent, four percent, and eight percent, respectively ($P < 0.05$) (Table 1). There were moderate relationships between increases in laboratory-based strength measurements and performance improvements for the overhead shot distance ($r = 0.60$), long jump distance ($r = 0.52$), and vertical jump height ($r = 0.61$).

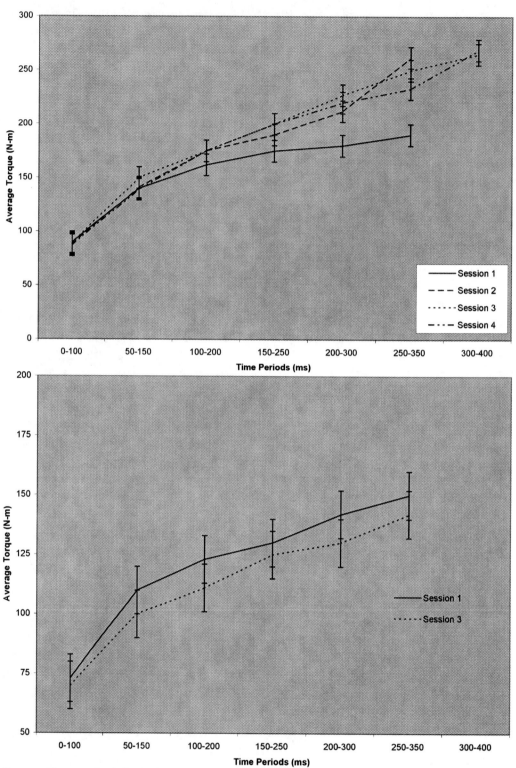

Figure 3. The rate of maximum force production in each test session for the athletes (a) and the controls (b). Rate of maximum force production represents the average torque calculated in 100 ms time periods from the onset of force production and overlapped by 50 ms. The normalization of the force-time curve across tests sessions is in the time domain to differentiate between improvements in maximal strength (high force portions of the absolute force-time curve) and rapid force production (early parts of the absolute force-time curve) (cf. Hakkinen, 1989). Error bars represent the standard errors of the means.

Discussion

The sport-specific resistance-training program improved the maximality of the neural drive during rapid isometric contractions, as indicated by the positive relationship between increases in MVC torques and increases in iEMG ($r = 0.63$). Specific to the peaking and maintenance phase, improvements to the pattern of neural drive were made evident by increases in EMG amplitudes at the onset of rapid isometric contractions. These results cannot exclude the possibility that other training regimens would produce similar results. The results also do not exclude the possibility that muscular adaptations contributed to strength gains and improved athletic performance. However, muscle twitch torques were unaffected, which tentatively suggests that neural adaptations were the predominant underlying mechanisms for the laboratory-based strength gains in these highly skilled athletes.

Most studies using the interpolated twitch technique to measure voluntary activation of the quadriceps muscle have reported values between 90 and 100 percent (cf. Behm and St. Pierre, 1998). Voluntary activation values of 72 percent, on average, probably represented potentiation bias during the MVC that was easily detected with a sensitive twitch interpolation technique. Twitch torque potentiation during the MVC would cause an underestimation of the "true" extent of voluntary activation (Belanger and McComas, 1981; Bulow et al., 1993). Voluntary activation of the quadriceps muscle was 83.0 ± 9.1 percent in healthy adults even when using a MVC lasting 10 s to measure post-activation potentiation of the resting muscle twitch (Hamada et al., 2000). Voluntary activation of the quadriceps muscle was between 85

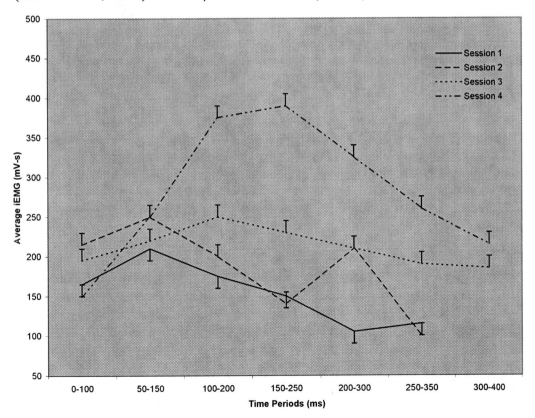

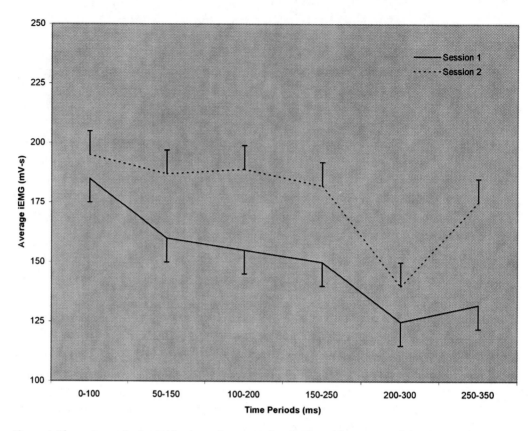

Figure 4. The pattern of neural drive in each test session for the athletes (a) and the controls (b). Pattern of neural drive represents the iEMG values expressed for 1 s, in each 100 ms time period from the onset of force production and overlapped by 50 ms. The normalization of the iEMG-time curve across test sessions is in the time domain to differentiate between improvements in maximal muscle activation (late part of the I-EMG-time curve) and muscle recruitment patterns during rapid movements (early parts of the iEMG-time curve) (cf. Hakkinen, 1989; iEMG expressed in absolute units). Error bars represent the standard errors of the means.

and 90 percent in both healthy controls and elite male volleyball players in the study of Huber *et al* (1998). Sport-specific resistance training did not induce increases in voluntary activation of the quadriceps muscle in our highly skilled athletes. This finding is in agreement with previous research on progressive resistance training in initially untrained individuals and in strength-trained athletes during taper procedures (Carolan and Cafarelli, 1992; Gibala *et al.*, 1994; Behm and St. Pierre, 1998; Herbert *et al.*, 1998).

There are inherently different underlying motor-control strategies for measuring neuromuscular performance during sustained MVC contractions and rapid MVC contractions. Torque-iEMG analyses of rapid isometric contractions at maximal effort provide additional insights on the voluntary activation of the agonist motonleuron pool, because of the limited capacity of the motor system to fully activate a muscle in a short time (Enokal, 1983; Gottlieb *et al.*, 1989; Suzuki *et al.*, 1994). The positive relationship between increases in MVC torques and increases in iEMG ($r = 0.63$) during the rapid isometric MVC task suggested that improvements to the maximality of neural drive may have occurred during the course of this sport-specific resistance-training program.

Improvements to the pattern of neural drive may manifest as increased motor-unit synchronization (Enoka, 1997). Although the evidence is not definitive, the hypothesis that increased motor-unit synchronization occurs with strength training is still tenable (Sale, 1988; Moritani, 1993, Enoka, 1997). Increasing motor-unit synchronization and motor-unit discharge rates are neural factors that contribute to increased surface-recorded EMG amplitude (Jones *et al.*, 1989; Moritani, 1993; Kamen and Knight, 1999; Yao *et al.*, 2000). The 71 percent increase in surface EMG amplitude is consistent with the effects of a moderate amount of motor-unit synchronization on reducing the cancellation of action potentials within the surface EMG signal. (Yao *et al.*, 2000). The training-induced increase in the averaged iEMG response at the onset of a rapid MVC may reflect a change in the motor-unit recruitment pattern—for example, increased synchronization or increased "doublets" firing. Alterations in the motor-unit recruitment pattern may improve the neuromuscular coordination underlying the technical aspects of athletic skill performance without a corresponding shift in the isometric torque-time curve. [For a discussion of the functional significance of motor-unit synchronization on isometric force, see Yao *et al.* (2000). For a discussion of the functional significance of motor-unit activation patterns on the speed of voluntary muscle contractions, see Van Cutsem *et al.* (1988).]

The observed increases in iEMG may be peripheral in origin (Jones et al., 1989; Narici et al., 1989; Herberty *et al.*, 1998). However, the concomitant increases in iEMG and MVC torque suggest that 16 weeks of sport-specific resistance training induces adaptations to neural drive. Previous research indicated that the magnitudes of strength adaptations for highly trained athletes were approximately five percent on average (Hakkinen *et al.*, 1987, 1988, 1991; Hakkinen and Pakarinen, 1991; Gibala *et al.*, 1994; Hekkinen and Kellinen, 1994). The magnitudes of strength adaptations observed in this research, 15 and 24 percent, were similar to values reported for individuals without a prolonged background in strength training (e.g., Narici *et al.*, 1989; Yue and Cole, 1992; Herbert *et al.*, 1998; Knight *et al.*, 1998; Akima *et al.*, 1999). Neural adaptations are considered to be the underlying mechanisms for the rapid strength gains in untrained individuals and for periodic strength gains in well-trained athletes, in whom the contributions of muscle hypertrophy may already be maximized (Enoka, 1988, 1997; Hakkinen, 1989; Jones *et al.*, 1989; Hakkinen and Kallinen, 1994; Kramer *et al.*, 1998; Sale, 1988). In addition, the transfer of performance improvements among the laboratory-based strength tasks and measurements of the overhead shot distance, long jump distance, and vertical jump height, as well as high athletic achievement, inferred that the sport-specific resistance-training program induced a motor learning adaptation (Jones *et al.*, 1989; Enoka, 1997). The reliability of iEMG values between sessions for the controls indicated that the EMG recording environment was consistent across days.

The strength-development phase induced the expected increase to the high-torque portion, greater than 200 ms, of the isometric torque-time curve (Hakkinen *et al.*, 1985a). An increase in musculotendinous stiffness after four weeks of progressive heavy-resistance exercise may explain the increase in torque per unit time in the absence of increased iEMG (Pousson *et al.*, 1990; Narici *et al.*, 1996). There was no subsequent increase in the high-velocity portion, less than 200 ms, of the isometric torque-time curve after either the strength-power phase or the peaking and maintenance phase (Hakkinen *et al.*, 1985b). Adaptations in the high-velocity portion of the isometric force-time curve depend upon an explosive type strength-training stimulus (Hakkinen, 1989). The hybrid nature or the short duration of the strength-power phase may not have provided our athletes with the most appropriate training stimulus to induce this adaptation.

In conclusion, our results support the hypothesis that sport-specific resistance training induces neural adaptations to the pattern of neural drive in highly skilled athletes. Although the sport-specific training program did not increase voluntary activation of the quadriceps muscle during a sustained MVC task, improvements to the maximality of neural drive may occur when the motor system is required to fully activate a muscle in a short time.

Acknowledgments

The authors are grateful to Drs Gary Kamen and Veronica Sciotti for providing comments on the manuscript.

References

Akima, H., Takahashi, H., Kuno, S.Y., Masuda, K., Masuda, T., Shimojo, H., Anno, I., Itai, Y., and Katsuta, S. (1999). Early phase adaptations of muscle use and strength to isokinetic training. *Medicine and Science in Sports and Exercise*, 31, 588-594.

Allen, G.M., Gandevia, S.C., and McKenzie, D.K. (1995). Reliability of measurements of muscle strength and voluntary activation using twitch interpolation. *Muscle and Nerve*, 18, 593-600.

Behm, D.G. and St. Pierre, D.M. (1998). The effects of strength training and disuse on the mechanisms of fatigue. *Sports Medicine*, 25, 173-189.

Belanger, A.Y. and McComas, A.J. (1981). Extent of motor unit activation during effort. *Journal of Applied Physiology*, 51, 1131-1135.

Bigland-Ritchie, B., Furbush, F., and Woods, J.J. (1986). Fatigue of intermittent submaximal voluntary contractions: central and peripheral factors. *Journal of Applied Physiology*, 61, 421-429.

Bulow, P.M., Norregaard, J., Danneskiold-Samsoe, B., and Mehlsen, J. (1993). Twitch interpolation technique in testing of maximal muscle strength: influence of potentiation, force level, stimulus intensity, and preload. *European Journal of Applied Physiology*, 67, 462-466.

Carolan, B. and Cafarelli, E. (1992). Adaptations in coactivation after isometric resistance training. *Journal of Applied Physiology*, 73, 911-917.

Edwards, R.H., Young, A., Hosking, G.P., and Jones, D.A. (1977). Human skeletal muscle function: description of tests and normal values. *Clinical Science and Molecular Medicine*, 52, 283-290.

Enoka, R.M. (1988). Muscle strength and its development: new perspectives. *Sports Medicine*, 6, 146-168.

Gibala, M.J., MacDougall, J.D., and Sale, D.G. (1994). The effects of tapering on strength performance in trained athletes. *International Journal of Sports Medicine*, 15, 492-497.

Gottlieb, G.L., Corcos, D.M., and Agarwal, G.C. (1989). Organizing principles for single-joint movements. A speed-insensitive strategy. *Journal of Neurophysiology*, 62, 342-357.

Hakkinen, K. (1989). Neuromuscular and hormonal adaptations during strength and power training: a review. *Journal of Sports Medicine and Physical Fitness*, 29, 9-26.

Hakkinen, K. and Kallinen, M. (1994). Distribution of strength-training volume into one or two daily sessions and neuromuscular adaptations in female athletes. *Electromyography and Clinical Neurophysiology*, 34, 117-124.

Hakkinen, K., and Pakarinen, A. (1991). Serum hormones in male strength athletes during intensive short-term strength training. *European Journal of Applied Physiology*, 63, 194-199.

Hakkinen, K., Alen, M., and Komi, P.V. (1985a). Changes in isometric force- and relaxation- time, electromyographic and muscle fiber characteristics of human skeletal muscle during strength training and detraining. *Acta Physiologica Scandinavica*, 125, 573-585.

Hakkinen, K., Komi, P.V., and Alen, M. (1985b). Effect of explosive type strength training on isometric force- and relaxation- time, electromyographic and muscle fiber characteristics of leg extensor muscles. *Acta Physiologica Scandinavica*, 125, 587-600.

Hakkinen, K., Komi, P.V., Alen, M., and Kauhanen, H. (1987). EMG, muscle fiber, and force production characteristics during a one-year training period in elite weightlifters. *European Journal of Applied Physiology*, 56, 419-427.

Hakkinen, K., Pakarinen, A., Alen, M., Kauhanen, H., and Komi, P.V. (1988). Neuromuscular and hormonal adaptations in athletes to strength training in two years. *Journal of Applied Physiology*, 65, 2406-2412.

Hakkinen, K., Kallinen, M., Komi, P.V., and Kauhanen, H. (1991). Neuromuscular adaptations during short-term "normal" and reduced training periods in strength athletes. *Electromyography and Clinical Neurophysiology*, 31, 35-42.

Hales, J.P. and Gandevia, S.C. (1988). Assessment of maximal voluntary contraction with twitch interpolation: an instrument to measure twitch responses. *Journal of Neuroscience Methods*, 25, 97-102.

Hamada, T., Sale, D.G., MacDougall, J.D., and Tarnopolsky, M.A. (2000). Postactivation potentiation, fiber type, and twitch contraction time in human knee extensor muscles. *Journal of Applied Physiology*, 88, 2131-2137.

Herbert, R.D., Dean, C., and Gandevia, S.C. (1988). Effects of real and imagined training on voluntary muscle activation during maximal isometric contractions. *Acta Physiologica Scandinavica*, 163, 361-368.

Huber, A., Suter, E., and Herzog, W. (1988). Inhibition of the quadriceps muscles in elite male volleyball players. *Journal of Sports Sciences*, 16, 281-289.

Jones, D.A., Rutherford, O.M., and Parker, D.F. (1989). Physiological changes in skeletal muscles as a result of strength training. *Quarterly Journal of Experimental Physiology*, 74, 233-256.

Judge, L.W. (1992). Preseason preparation for the collegiate shot putter. *National Strength and Conditioning Association Journal*, 14, 20-26.

Kamen, G. and Knight, C.A. (1999). The relationship between maximal motor unit firing rate and surface-recorded EMG amplitude in young and older adults. In *Proceedings of the Fifth International Brain Research Organization World Congress of Neuroscience*, p. 67, Paris: IBRO.

Kaman, G., Knight, C.A., Laroche, D.P., and Asermely, D.G. (1989). Resistance training increases vastus lateralis motor unit firing rates in young and older adults. *Medicine and Science in Sports and Exercise*, 30 (suppl. 5), 337.

Knight, C.A., Kamen, G., and Burke, J.R. (1998). Increased motor unit activation in young and older adults following resistance exercise training. *Medicine and Science in Sports and Exercise*, 30 (suppl. 5), 336.

Koceja, D.M., Bernacki, R.H., and Kamen, G. (1991). Methodology for the quantitative assessment of human crossed- spinal reflex pathways. *Medical and Biological Engineering and Computing*, 29, 603-606.

Kramer, W.J., Duncan, N.D., and Volek, J.S. (1998). Resistance training and elite athletes: adaptations and program considerations. *Journal of Orthopaedic and Sports Physical Therapy*, 28, 110-119.

Moritani, T. (1993). Neuromuscular adaptations during the acquisition of muscle strength, power, and motor tasks. *Journal of Biomechanics*, 26 (suppl. 1), 95-107.

Narici, M.V., Roi, G.S., Landoni, L., Minetti, A.E., and Cerretelli, P. (1989). Changes in force, cross-sectional area, and neural activation during strength training and detraining of the human quadriceps. *European Journal of Applied Physiology*, 59, 310-319.

Narici, M.V., Hoppeler, H., Kayser, B., Landoni, L., Claassen, H., Gavardi, C., Conti, M., and Cerretelli, P. (1996). Human quadriceps cross-sectional area, torque, and neural activation during six months strength training. *Acta Physiologica Scandinavica*, 157, 175-186.

Pousson, M., Van Hoecke, J., and Goubel, F. (1990). Changes in elastic characteristics of human muscle induced by eccentric exercise. *Journal of Biomechanics*, 23, 343-348.

Sale, D.G. (1988). Neural adaptation to resistance training. *Medicine and Science in Sports and Exercise*, 20, 135-145.

Suzuki, M., Yamazaki, Y., and Matsunami, K. (1994). Relationship between force and electromyographic activity during rapid isometric contraction in power grip. *Electroencephalography and Clinical Neurophysiology*, 93, 218-224.

Van Cutsem, M., Duchateau, J., and Hainaut, K. (1998). Changes in single motor unit behavior contribute to the increase in contraction speed after dynamic training in humans. *Journal of Physiology (London)*, 513 (Part 1), 295-305.

Yao, W., Fuglevand, R.J., and Enoka, R.M. (2000). Motor-unit synchronization increases EMG amplitude and decreases force steadiness of simulated contractions. *Journal of Neurophysiology*, 83, 441-452.

Yue, G. and Cole, K.J. (1992). Strength increases from the motor program: comparison of training with maximal voluntary and imagined muscle contractions. *Journal of Neurophysiology*, 67, 1114-1123.

22
Medicine Ball Functional Training

By Rob Lasorsa

To be successful in today's track and field environment, athletes must work on a variety of components of athletic ability. Flexibility, strength, speed, power, agility, balance, technique, kinesthetic awareness, endurance, psychological development, and injury prevention are all areas that need improvement for an individual to become a successful athlete. As individuals become more athletic, their performances will comparably improve.

Because of time restraints, an athlete will usually only concentrate on one or two aspects. For example, a discus thrower may only work on strength (by spending a great deal of time in the weight room) and technique (by taking a large volume of throws). In this scenario, the discus thrower is bypassing many significant training areas that are equally important to their success. As a result, their optimum performance level is never fulfilled.

It is virtually impossible to select each individual component of athletic ability and improve each component by isolating activities for just that area.

It is virtually impossible to select each individual component of athletic ability and improve each component by isolating activities for just that area. There is simply not enough time. Therefore, coaches and athletes must engage in activities that will "cross train" many areas at the same time. This factor underlies the importance of medicine ball "functional" training.

Fortunately, several drills exist that will enable the athlete to work on many components of athletic ability at the same time, including balance, kinesthetic awareness, agility, speed and power, strength, endurance, and flexibility. Furthermore, a proper training program "housing" all these areas of athletic ability will decrease the possibility of injuries.

Medicine balls come in a variety of sizes and weights. In most cases, athletes should start out with lighter balls, and as they achieve higher athletic ability levels, the weight of the medicine balls they utilize should be increased.

The standard "rule of thumb" is to always use a ball whose weight allows the correct technique of the drill to be performed. Using a ball that is too heavy will cause a breakdown in skills. Sets, reps, and recovery time are also important and are specific to the athlete's individual needs. Too many sets or reps, or not enough recovery time, can cause fatigue and improper skill performance. In general, the use of basic sets and reps is recommended. For example, three sets of eight reps or four sets of six reps is an excellent point to begin. It is also essential to perform each drill with both sides of the body.

> Too many sets or reps, or not enough recovery time, can cause fatigue and improper skill performance.

Medicine Balls That Are Recommended and Why

☐ *First-place medicine balls:*
- Bounce well and are great for working out alone or with others
- Inflate more for a higher bounce
- Textured surface provides an excellent grip
- Ranges from volleyball to basketball in size, as the weight of the ball increases

☐ *First-place core balls:*
- Two handles make it excellent for core and torso work.
- Can be thrown against wall to develop power or on field for distance throws.
- All weights are 11 inches in diameter.

☐ *Nemo medicine balls:*
- Compact—easy to grip and throw
- Less bounce than the first-place med ball
- Smaller balls (one, two, three kg) are approximately volleyball size
- Larger balls (four, five, six, seven, eight kg) are slightly larger than basketball size

☐ *Converta-balls:*
- Use with a rope for swinging, chopping, and rotational drills.
- Use without a rope as a traditional med ball.
- Bounces well—inflate for higher bounce
- Ball diameter increases proportionally with weight.

☐ *Power balls:*
- Grasp the handle for rotary drills, dumbbell simulation, and throwing and running movements.
- Improve explosive power by throwing underhand, overhand, or sidearm.
- Soft, does not bounce
- All weights are the same size.

☐ *D-Balls:*
- Soft and easy to grip, catch, and throw
- Do not bounce
- Diameter ranges from 3.5 inches to 10.6 inches, from smallest to heaviest weight

Suggested Medicine Ball Drills

☐ *Modified hammer throw.* Start with the ball on the hip opposite of the throw/delivery side. Start transferring the weight from the backside to the delivery side by turning the back foot, while twisting the body's core. Finish by throwing/delivering the ball at shoulder height, with your weight balanced over the delivery side. This throw can also begin at shoulder height, instead of by the hip.

☐ *Side throws.* Begin at 90 degrees to the wall, with the ball on the hip, and more weight on that leg. Deliver the ball at hip height, with the weight now transferred to the front leg. Catch the ball and repeat.

☐ *Puts.* Start with the ball behind one hip, with more weight on that leg. Throw ("put") the ball, while turning and reaching towards the direction of the throw. Finish the drill in a balanced position.

☐ *Russian twist.* Start with the ball at belly-button height, arms-length away from the body, behind the right or left hip. Start by moving the ball to the right or left. Keep the core tight and turn/rotate your back foot to allow greater range of motion.

☐ *Single leg Russian twist.* Same as above, but when the weight is off of the back leg, take it off of the ground.

☐ *Diagonal chops.* Start with the ball behind and above the ear. Move the ball diagonally across the body, ending near the opposite knee. Return with the same pattern. Rotate/turn the back foot to increase the effective range of exercise.

☐ *Single leg chop.* Same as diagonal chops, but balance on one leg, while performing the exercise.

☐ *Chops.* Start with the ball overhead at arms length. Chop down and stop when the ball is between your feet.

☐ *Figure 8s.* Begin with the ball at ear level, but with the arms extended away from the body. Move the ball through a figure-8 pattern continuously—in front of and beside your body from left to right.

☐ *Circles.* Begin with the ball overhead and move the ball in a circular motion as big as possible around your body.

☐ *Med ball squat.* Keep the ball at arms length, while performing a squat. A variation: start with the ball at the chest and press up or out when squatting, returning the ball to the chest on ascent.

☐ *One leg squat.* Begin with the ball at arms length, straight in front of the body. Squat on one leg, keeping the ball held out in front as a counterbalance. Leave the free leg in front. (You can also leave the free leg to the side or the rear.) Variation: the ball can start from the belly button and be pressed out when squatting.

☐ *Med ball lunge I.* Begin with the ball at the belly-button level. Take a step forward with one leg, while moving the ball to the side of the lunging leg. Continue alternating legs by either walking or switching in place.

☐ *Med ball lunge II.* Begin with the ball at the belly button. While lunging forward, raise the ball up overhead. Either leave the ball overhead while continuing to lunge or return the ball to the belly button on each lunge.

☐ *Sagittal or front reach.* Begin with the ball at the belly button. Step forward and extend the arms towards the front foot. Return and repeat in place with the same foot or alternate feet.

☐ *Frontal or side reach.* Begin with the ball at the belly button. Step and reach laterally to one side. Continue reaching and stepping to one side or alternating legs.

☐ *Transverse or rear reach.* Begin with the ball at the belly button. Open (turn) and step/reach between 90 and 180 degrees to the rear. Return to the start and repeat with the same leg or opposite leg.

☐ *Med ball pushup.* Position the ball under one hand and perform a pushup. Try doing one pushup with the hand on the ground, pushing hard enough to catch yourself on the ball for the next rep. Begin to roll the ball across to the opposite hand between reps if you want a bigger challenge.

☐ *Two-arm wall pass.* Begin facing the wall about an arm's length away. Keep the hands above the head, initially keeping the throwing range short. Work towards the arms being bent and further away from the wall. You can also do this with one arm only.

☐ *Slams.* Begin with the ball overhead. Throw the ball down, using your core. You can also perform this drill with one arm only.

☐ *Knee throw to pushup.* Begin on the knees, with the ball in front of the chest. Throw the ball forward and follow it with the upper body. When your body extension is complete, catch yourself in a pushup position. This drill can also be initiated from an overhead-ball position.

Andy Lyons/Getty Images Sport

To be successful in the current track and field competitive environment, athletes must work on a variety of components of athletic ability.

☐ *Wall throws.* Stand six-to-eight feet from the wall. Swing the ball to an overhead position, stretching the upper extremities. Throw the ball, aiming one-to-two feet above the bottom of the wall, using your core.

☐ *One-step wall throws.* Start with the ball at the belly button. Swing the ball to an overhead position and step forward with one foot towards the wall. Shift the weight completely over the front throwing leg, using your core to throw the ball. Aim one-to-two feet above the bottom of the wall.

☐ *Squat throw.* Start with the ball at the chest or overhead. Quickly squat, lowering the ball to calf level. Jump and throw the ball as high as possible directly overhead. Let the ball bounce once, reposition, and repeat the drill.

☐ *Over-the-back toss.* Start with the ball overhead and bring it forward and down to the knees. Begin the throw as soon as the ball gets to the knee level. Throw by extending the ankle, knee, and hip, and delivering the ball overhead backwards, keeping the toes on the ground. This drill is a great total-body power test.

☐ *Single-arm throw. (great with the core ball or power ball).* Start in a bent position, holding the ball with one hand between the feet. Throw the ball as high as possible, straight overhead (not backwards) by extending at the knee, ankle, and hip. The ball should move close to the body for best height.

23

Shot Put Glide Technique

By Rob Lasorsa

* All movements are based on a right-handed thrower.

Grip, Carry, Release

☐ *Grip:*

- Objective: Proper placement of shot in hand

- Description: The shot is placed on the "ball" of the hand. The fingers are slightly spread and placed behind the shot, while the thumb is placed on the side of the implement for control.

☐ *Carry:*

- Objective: Proper placement of shot against the neck

- Description: The shot is placed under the chin and against the neck, above the clavicle. The hand is "behind" the shot, not underneath it.

☐ *Throw into the ground:*

- Objective: Proper arm extension and hand "follow through"

- Description: Bend at the waist so that the upper body is parallel to the ground. Place the non-throwing hand under the shot and the throwing hand on top of the shot. The elbows should be out. Starting from the chest, the shot is "pushed" to the ground by fully extending the throwing arm. The fingers of the throwing hand should "follow through."

☐ *Kneeling throw #1:*

- Objective: Proper arm extension and hand "follow through"

- Description: Facing the throwing direction, place the right knee on the ground. The left arm is extended towards the throwing direction. From its proper position against the neck, the shot is "pushed" in the throwing direction, using correct arm extension and wrist action.

> When gripping the shot, the shot should be placed on the "ball" of the hand.

☐ *Kneeling throw #2:*

- Objective: Proper throwing arm and non-throwing arm action
- Description: During the throwing movement of the kneeling throw #1 drill, allow the non-throwing hand to come towards the non-throwing shoulder. Do not allow the shoulders to rotate.

☐ *Kneeling throw #3:*

- Objective: Proper throwing-arm action from a longer push position
- Description: Starting in the same position as in the kneeling throw #1 drill, rotate the shoulders 90 degrees to the right so that the shot is behind the right hip. "Push" the ball in the throwing direction as in the previous drill. The shoulders will naturally come to the front without forcefully rotating.

Sequence of Movement

☐ *Kneel to stand #1:*

- Objective: Concept of throwing from the "ground on up" (using the lower body before the upper body)
- Description: From the kneeling throw #1 drill position, stand up by fully extending the legs. Execute a proper release from this position.

☐ *Kneel to stand #2:*

- Objective: Concept of using the lower body before the upper body from a longer "push" position
- Description: From the kneeling throw #3 drill position, stand up, while keeping the shot behind the right hip and upper body 90 degrees to the right. Execute a proper release from this position.

Power Position

☐ *Right-foot turn #1:*

- Objective: Proper movement of the right foot
- Description: Stand 90 degrees to the right of the throwing direction, with the shot placed against the neck and the non-throwing arm extended. Turn the right foot inward (which will cause the right hip to face towards the throwing direction), while keeping the upper body in its original place.

☐ *Right-foot turn #2:*

- Objective: Proper movement of the right foot
- Description: Perform the same action as in the right-foot turn #1 drill. Execute a release after the right foot cannot turn anymore.

☐ *Lower-body turn:*

- Objective: Proper turning movement of the lower body

When throwing the shot, the sequence of movement involves throwing from the "ground on up" (using the lower body before the upper body)

- Description: From the right-foot turn #1 drill starting position, rotate the upper body and left foot an additional 90 degrees to the right. The right foot remains in its original position. From this position, the right foot initiates the movement by turning inward. Keep the upper body "back" as long as possible, so that the lower body can "lead" the throw. Once the lower body is turned to the front, and the left foot is firmly planted on the ground, execute a release.

☐ *Right-leg extension:*

- Objective: Proper right-leg extension

- Description: From the right-foot turn #1 drill position, lower the body over the right foot by bending the right leg. The only part of the left foot that is in contact with the ground should be the big toe. Extend the right leg without turning the right foot.

☐ *Side-standing throw:*

- Objective: Proper sequence of movements

- Description: From a side-power position, forcefully extend the right leg, while the right foot is turning inward. Feel the legs and hips work independently of the upper body. Once the lower body is fully extended and turned to the front, execute a release, while the left foot is firmly planted on the ground.

☐ *Full-standing throw:*

- Objective: Proper sequence of movement from the power position

- Description: From the side-standing throw drill position, rotate the upper body an additional 90 degrees to the right. The right foot remains in its original position. Execute the same movement, with the lower body as in the side-standing throw drill. Perform a proper release at the front.

> In the sequence of movement, once the lower body is fully extended and turned to the front, execute a release, while the left foot is firmly planted on the ground.

Michael Steele/Getty Images Sport

Movement Across Ring

☐ *Left-leg extension #1:*

- Objective: Maintain proper weight distribution

- Description: From the full-standing throw drill position, bring the left foot next to the right. Extend the left leg back to its original position, while keeping the shoulders back. Do not shift weight towards the front, as the left leg is extending.

☐ *Left-leg extension #2:*

- Objective: Proper movement once the left foot touches the ground

- Description: Execute the same movement as in the left-leg extension #1 drill. Once the left foot touches, perform a standing throw from the power position. Allow for continual movement without a hesitation in the power position.

☐ *Backwards walk #1:*

- Objective: Backwards movement

- Description: From the right-foot turn #2 drill position, walk backwards. Keep the shoulders back as the lower body stays "active" (90 degrees).

☐ *Backwards walk #2:*

- Objective: Backwards movement, while staying low

- Description: While keeping the knees bent, execute the same movement as in the backwards walk #1 drill.

☐ *Backwards step #1:*

- Objective: Backwards movement into the power position

- Description: From the right-foot turn #2 drill position, lower into the legs. Step back with the left. Pull the right leg underneath the upper body and then extend the left leg towards the front of the ring, so that a power position is obtained. Keep the shoulders back during the whole drill.

☐ *Backwards step #2:*

- Objective: Backwards movement into a throw

- Description: Execute the same movement as in the backwards step #1 drill. Once the left foot touches in the front of the circle, perform a standing throw from the power position. Allow for continual movement without any hesitation in the power position.

The backwards hop drill #1 helps develop the ability to move explosively backwards.

☐ *Backwards hop #1:*

- Objective: Explosive backwards movement

- Description: From the backwards step #1 drill position, step back with the left foot, hop into the air off the left foot, pull the right leg underneath the upper body, and extend the left leg in order to land in a proper power position.

☐ *Backwards hop #2:*
- Objective: Explosive backwards movement into a throw
- Description: Execute the same movement as in the backwards hop #1 drill. Once the left foot touches at the front of the circle, perform a standing throw from the power position. Allow for continual movement without any hesitation in the power position. Stay in a "double-support" base (do not reverse) once the shot is released.

☐ *Backwards step #3:*
- Objective: Turning the lower body to an "active" position while moving
- Description: Starting at the back of the ring, face the back with both feet together. The shot is placed properly against the neck, and the non-throwing arm is extended. Step back with the right foot, while turning it inward 90 degrees. Bring the left foot to the front of the circle, while sinking over the right leg in order to obtain a proper power position.

☐ *Backwards step #4:*
- Objective: Turning the lower body to an "active" position and continuing into a throw
- Description: Execute the same movement as in the backwards step #3 drill and continue into a throw once a power position it properly obtained.

Glide

☐ *One-foot hop on line:*
- Objective: Turning the right foot
- Description: Balance on the right foot, while standing on a line. Take a small, backward hop off the right foot, while staying on the line. Each time a hop occurs, turn the right foot inwards 90 degrees to get the right leg and hip in an "active" position. The shoulders should stay back, while the right foot is turning.

☐ *Fence drill #1:*
- Objective: Keep the upper body back, while the lower body becomes "active"
- Description: Hold onto a fence with both hands. The arms are outstretched. Balance on the right foot. Hop upwards off the right foot, turning both hips 90 degrees while in the air. Bend the right knee at landing in order to achieve a power position.

☐ *Fence drill #2:*
- Objective: Keep the upper body back, while the lower body becomes "active"
- Description: Start in the same position as in fence drill #1, except place the shot against the neck and only hold onto the fence with the non-throwing hand. Perform the same action as in the previous drill.

The fence drill #1 is designed to help the thrower keep the upper body back, while the lower body becomes "active".

- ☐ *Fence drill #3:*
  - Objective: Left-leg extension
  - Description: Start in the same position as in fence drill #2. Bring the left knee next to the right knee and then extend it back to its starting position.
- ☐ *Fence drill #4:*
  - Objective: Start of movement at the back of the ring
  - Description: Start in the same position as in fence drill #3. Again, bring the left knee next to the right knee, while simultaneously bending the right knee so that the hips are moving back and down slightly.
- ☐ *Fence drill #5:*
  - Objective: Beginner's glide movement
  - Description: Start and perform the same movements as in fence drill #4. Once in the slightly-seated position, simultaneously extend the left leg back towards the ground and hop upwards off the right foot. Turn the lower body 90 degrees in order to get it "active." As the right foot lands, allow the body weight to sink over a bent right knee so that a power position is achieved. Hold onto the fence during the whole action.
- ☐ *Fence drill #6:*
  - Objective: Beginner's glide movement to a throw
  - Description: Perform fence drill #5. Once in the power position, let go of the fence and take a standing throw.
- ☐ *Glide stop:*
  - Objective: Glide movement
  - Description: Start at the back of the ring and perform an action similar to fence drill #4. This time, the right foot will hop slightly up and back. Once the right leg is extended, "pull" the right knee back underneath the upper body in order to land in a correct power position. Both feet should land on the ground approximately at the same time (the right foot may land slightly before the left foot).
- ☐ *Glide, stop, and throw:*
  - Objective: Glide movement to a throw
  - Description: Perform the glide-stop drill. After landing in the power position, take a standing throw.
- ☐ *Full throw:*
  - Objective: A full throw
  - Description: Perform the glide, stop, and throw drill without hesitating in the power position. As soon as the feet land in the power position, proper action of the lower body must take place, while keeping the shoulders back as long as possible. Stay in a "double-support" base (do not reverse) after the release.

When performing a full throw, as soon as the feet land in the power position, proper action of the lower body must take place, while keeping the shoulders back as long as possible.

24

The ABCs of Footwork

By Steve Myrland

Improving footwork for sport performance offers the collateral benefit of reducing injury potential, since enhanced control of the center of gravity in motion will do the same for the human body that upgrading the engine, brakes, and suspension of a car does for the performance of the vehicle. It is also useful to consider that the "physical education" programs in many (most) American school systems are anything but physical and educational. The end result is, too often, human bodies trying to acquire complex sport-movement skills before mastering basic movement abilities. (Who, among the coaches reading this, has not encountered the all-star wonder kid player, only to discover that individual is unable to skip?) Teaching a progression of quantifiable and qualifiedly movement skills with integrated upper-, middle-, and lower-body mechanics is a fun and relatively easy part of training.

My primary tool for footwork training is the ABC (agility, balance, and coordination) ladder (my version of the agility ladder). It is worth noting that I decided to make my own ladder after being both entranced with the possibilities of ladder training and frustrated by the limitations of the ladders I was using. This article is not intended as a commercial for the ABC version. Rather, it is intended as a strong recommendation to give any ladder a place in your training program.

Footwork Training

Develop a repertoire of exercises the way you would go about expanding any training concept: in a carefully drawn progression of drills going from simple to complex, and increasing the speed of any drill only after you have mastered it at a slow, controlled pace. The ideal way to build this repertoire of exercises is to work on perfecting three or four movements in a training session, reviewing these movements in subsequent sessions, and adding an additional drill or two as you go. The drills you choose to include should reflect identifiable, sport-specific movements. This step enables you to easily relate the training to the sport—a factor that always speeds the learning curve along.

> Teaching a progression of quantifiable and qualifiedly movement skills with integrated upper-, middle-, and lower-body mechanics is a fun and relatively easy part of training.

A simple way to add greater strength and proprioceptive demands to an ABC ladder session is to place the ladder on a gentle hill.

Changing the Training Demand

A simple way to add greater strength and proprioceptive demands to an ABC ladder session is to place the ladder on a gentle hill. In this scenario, you will have to work against resistance when you move up the hill; and you will have the assistance of the hill when you come back down.

One drill involving a hill which can incorporate a ladder is the three-count shuffle.* A simple drill like the three-count shuffle has additional options from which to choose. For example, facing forward when you move up the hill gives you the increased resistance; coming down backwards forces you to move and be balanced at a slightly faster pace than normal, because the hill's gradient causes you to accelerate. You can reverse the effect simply by working backward up the hill, and forward down the hill. Then, rotate the resistance/assistance within each repetition. If your right shoulder is pointing up the hill, you will face resistance each time you push off of your left foot and extra eccentric loading on that foot as you decelerate your return off the right.

Using an ABC ladder can help you move faster, better, and safer. By keeping these simple ideas in mind, athletes can acquire even more complex movement skills through ladder training, and the learning can come surprisingly fast.

The ladder, then, can be a gratifying element of training for sports, where acquiring new skills is generally a long and difficult process.

Ronald Martinez/Getty Images Sport

Improving footwork for sport performance offers collateral benefit of reducing injury potential.

Training Tips

The following are some simple guidelines to keep in mind while learning ladder drills:

- *Go as fast as you can, not as fast as you can't.* The idea is to complete the drill correctly, rather than trip and drag the ladder halfway through, because you are attempting to go at a speed at which you cannot control your movements.

- *Rhythm before tempo.* Find the rhythm or meter of the drill, and hear your feet achieving that rhythm before you attempt to increase the tempo (pace) of the exercise.

- *Word cues.* If the rhythm eludes you, use word cues (i.e., in-in-out, in-in-out) and be sure to say them out loud. Trust me on this—feet are hard of hearing, but they will do what they are told if you actually speak the cues.

- *Most athletes are completely unaware of what their arms are doing while they are concentrating on where their feet are going.* The coach must facilitate the inclusion of the upper body. Always pay attention to what an athlete's arms are (or are not) doing. In all cases, arm movements must be integrated with foot movements (and facilitated by strength and stability through the body's core). Learning drills as simple foot-placement exercises without including proper arm mechanics will not produce functional results.

> In all cases, arm movements must be integrated with foot movements (and facilitated by strength and stability through the body's core).

* Three-count shuffle (forward): Stand just to the left of the ladder, facing along its length. Step into the first space with your right foot; step in with your left foot; step out to the right side of the ladder with your right foot; and repeat the other way. The rhythm is waltz-like: *one*-two-three, *one*-two-three…and the word cues are *in*-in-out, *in*-in-out or *right*-left-right, *left*-right-left.

25

Body Awareness and Building Athleticism... Training for Success

By Joe Napoli

Balance, core strength, and body awareness are critical areas that are often overlooked when building a solid training program.

During my many years of coaching athletes in various sports, I have come to the conclusion that the major of athletes do not know how their bodies work or, more importantly, how their bodies should feel when in motion. Balance, core strength, and body awareness are critical areas that are often overlooked when building a solid training program. It's alarming how many throwers never learn how to train properly. Many think just by picking up an implement and taking throw after throw is the answer to increasing distance. As coaches, we know that the act of just throwing does not adequately challenge the physical requirements necessary to elevate an athlete to a higher level of performance. Not learning proper techniques can not only lead to injury, boredom, and burnout, but possibly an end to a promising athletic future. How do we expect throwers to pick up implements, some heavy I might add, and throw them as far as they can when they do not even know how they should be feeling?

Athletes involved in a well-planned conditioning program are at a distinct advantage in reaching their full athletic potential. Not surprisingly, by establishing a strong foundation of sound training principles provides athletes with a better chance of obtaining higher levels of athletic performance. It can also improve their levels of self-esteem and confidence and decrease their potential for injuries.

The point that needs to be emphasized is that coaches need to make training fun and purposeful. Athletes need to be taught proper techniques and be made aware of the fact that it's OK to make mistakes, as long as they learn from them. An effort needs to be undertaken to build the level of core strength of all athletes and start teaching them what it takes to become athletic.

The focus of any program should be to educate the athlete, while building athleticism. There is a story I always use with my kids. When we are born, we first sit up and *crawl*; then, we eventually establish some type of balance, so we stand up and *walk*; and finally, when our bodies are perfectly in tune and we have great confidence, we *run*. This scenario sums up perfectly the proper procedure for training for success. The following should be incorporated into every sound training program:

☐ *Fitness testing.* Fitness testing should be the main part of any training program. In fact, it should be the foundation on which a successful training program is built. Athletes need to learn the importance of challenging themselves through a variety of different tests. Testing should be performed at least every three months (e.g., SLJ, SVJ, STJ, 3-hop, 4-hop, 30M, sit and reach, and medicine ball throws—front, back, overhead, squat, PC, snatch, incline, bench, etc.).

☐ *Developmental regimen.* Between each testing phase, you should have your athletes work on balance and stability, flexibility, core strength, SAQ, power, strength, and plyometrics. Fitness testing should be done again after 12 weeks in order to identify an athlete's strengths and weaknesses. This schedule will enable your athletes to see the progress they have made and to set goals for themselves.

☐ *Keep an eye on the prize.* The ultimate goal of this program is to teach the athlete the importance of body awareness and how it relates to them in improving their throws. Remember to always keep your athletes motivated and have fun while training and competing.

Coaches need to make training fun and purposeful.

Mike Powell/Getty Images Sport

26

Ten Negative Side Effects of Taking Steroids

By James A. Peterson, Ph.D., FACSM

1. *Heightened risk of injury.* Individuals who increase their level of muscular strength and size by taking anabolic steroids may be exposed to an elevated risk of injuring their tendons and ligaments. Such a risk is caused, in part, by the fact that muscle tissue strengthens faster than connective tissue, and, to a degree, the tendons and ligaments can't accommodate quickly enough.

2. *Unbecoming conduct.* Steroid use has been linked to increased levels of aggressive behavior. The extent of the impact that steroids have on an individual's mood and actions depends on a number of factors, including the type of anabolic steroids used, the size and frequency of the steroids doses, how long a person takes steroids, and how a person takes steroids (e.g., orally or by injection).

Research has found that steroid use raises the cholesterol level in an individual's blood.

3. *Increased potential for heart disease.* Research has found that steroid use raises the cholesterol level in an individual's blood. Oral anabolic steroids have been shown to dramatically decrease the level of HDL-C (the "good" cholesterol) and increase the level of LDL-C (the "bad" cholesterol) in the blood, thereby substantially raising a person's risk of coronary heart disease.

4. *Beleaguered complexion.* Individuals who use steroids frequently suffer from acne. Steroids can cause an individual's oil glands to enlarge and secrete more frequently. In turn, the excess secretion can clog the pores of the skin, resulting in unsightly changes in a steroid user's complexion.

5. *Blood clots.* Steroids could cause the platelets in the blood to be more likely to stick together. By increasing the likelihood for the formation of blood clots, steroids increase a person's chances of having a heart attack resulting from a blood clot in the coronary arteries.

6. *Arrested development.* Adolescents who take steroids can experience premature closure of the epiphyscal (growth) plates. As such, taking steroids can cause children to have stunted growth.

7. *Liver toxicity.* Because the liver is the principle site for steroid clearance for individuals who take anabolic steroids orally, an excessive intake of steroids can be toxic to the liver. As a result, the liver can become vulnerable to serious damage, such as cysts and tumors. This damage can develop relatively rapidly after a person consumes a substantial amount of steroids, or it may develop gradually over a period of years as a result of prolonged consumption of small amounts of potentially toxic substances, such as steroids.

8. *Hair today, gone tomorrow.* Steroids use may result in hair loss. For example, men prone to baldness may lose their hair faster. Concurrently (or separately), steroid users may also experience an increase in their level of body hair (in areas other than on their scalp).

> By increasing the likelihood for the formation of blood clots, steroids increase a person's chances of having a heart attack resulting from a blood clot in the coronary arteries.

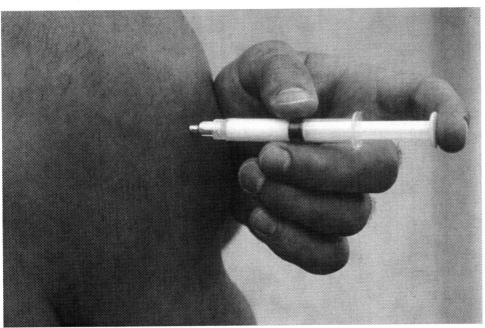

Karen Levy/Getty Images Sport

Taking steroids has a number of potentially harmful side effects.

Long-term anabolic steroid abuse has been associated with causing a man to have a diminished sexual desire.

9. *Temporary blanks.* Long-term anabolic steroid abuse has been associated with causing a man to have a diminished sexual desire. In addition to affecting a man's interest in sex, steroids can have an impact on his reproductive system in other negative ways, including causing his testicles to atrophy, lowering his production of sperm, and reducing the level of several of his essential reproductive hormones.

10. *Masculinizing effects.* Similar to their male counterparts, steroids have also been shown to have serious side effects for women. For example, depending upon the frequency of use and dosage levels, taking steroids will cause most women to exhibit an enhanced level of male characteristics, including a deepening of the voice, an increase in the amount of facial hair, and the development of a more "manly" body shape. In addition, steroids can cause a woman's breasts to shrink and her menstrual cycle to be disrupted. In men, however, steroids can have a feminizing effect (e.g., the development of breast-like tissue).

27

Treating Back Pain: Understanding the Basics

By James A. Peterson, Ph.D., FACSM

"Primum non nocere." (First of all, do no harm.) – Hippocrates

The statistics on back pain present an extraordinarily bleak picture: over 10 million sufferers annually, over 100 million workdays lost every year, over five billion dollars in direct and indirect treatment costs, and bouts of pain and intolerable anguish so seemingly countless as to give new meaning to the term "implausible." And yet, for all of the world's technological advances, for all of the evolutionary advances in the body of medical knowledge relating to pain, a simple fact remains: the mysteries of back pain often defy simple solutions. It is somewhat easier to explain why this is so than to accept the explanation. *At best, medicine is not an exact science.* If it were, surely a world in which the means were created for travel among the stars of the outer reaches of the universe would find a way to identify a foolproof method of treating (and preventing) back pain.

At best, medicine is not an exact science.

Not surprisingly, considerable debate exists within the medical community on how to effectively treat back pain. This article presents an overview of the most typical approaches and means for treating back pain. For discussion purposes, the possible therapies are divided into two groups: nonsurgical and surgical.

Nonsurgical Therapies

First, the good news. Your chances of not needing surgery to treat your back condition are excellent. Most back pain can be eliminated through one or a combination of any of the various nonsurgical back therapies that have been identified over the years. In fact, the need for much of the back surgery currently conducted has been subject to considerable questioning. Now, the bad news. There are no guarantees—no treatment, surgical or nonsurgical, can guarantee elimination of your back pain.

Physicians have found that most of the nonsurgical therapies discussed in this section have a 60-to-70 percent chance of being successful. Which one should you use? This is something that you should discuss with your doctor. In fact, were you to check with several different physicians, it is likely that you would receive several different pieces of advice. The best advice you could be given is to try two or three of the nonsurgical treatment options. If your back pain persists after your nonsurgical efforts, it is then time to consider other alternatives.

> If your back pain persists after your nonsurgical efforts, it is then time to consider other alternatives.

☐ Bed Rest

Lying in bed (except for an occasional visit to the bathroom) is the most commonly prescribed treatment for back pain, particularly in the acute phase. Bed rest is frequently effective because it reduces the mechanical irritation of your spine and diminishes the level of inflammation in the area surrounding the irritation. As a result, nature (vis-à-vis bed rest) may enable you to become pain-free without any additional action on your part. There are at least two possible problems, however, with bed rest therapy. First, it doesn't work for everyone. In fact, some individuals find that their back pain is aggravated by lying down. Second, most individuals don't have the time or patience to spend two to three weeks in bed. All too clearly, they realize that whatever factor initially caused their back pain is likely to do so again in the not-too-distant future. Despite these potential problems, bed rest is the oldest, and possibly the most widely prescribed, therapy for treating back pain.

☐ Drug Therapy

Drug therapy is another commonly accepted therapy for treating back pain. The most widely used drug is aspirin. Aspirin serves as both a painkiller and an anti-inflammatory to reduce the effect of the actual injury. Most physicians recommend that you take the maximum dose (three aspirin every four hours) as soon as possible after the onset of your back pain. Other drugs which, in addition to aspirin, are classified as "painkillers" include aspirin-like drugs (e.g., Tylenol) and certain narcotics (e.g., codeine, morphine, Demerol, Darvon, and Percodan).

Muscle relaxants comprise the second category of drugs sometimes prescribed for the treatment of back pain. This type of drug is only available through a doctor's prescription. Among the well-known muscle relaxants are Flexoril, Valium, Norflex, and Robaxin. Although such drugs have been known to help some individuals, most reputable physicians are reluctant to prescribe them for the treatment of back pain because the possible negative effects outweigh the possible benefits.

The third classification of drugs that are often used to treat back pain is anti-inflammatory medicine. Generally, this type of drug is recommended for individuals who need an anti-inflammatory but for whom aspirin has an undesirable side effect. A listing of anti-inflammatory drugs includes: Motrin, Indocin, Butazolidone, Clinoril, Feldene, and Tolectin.

The precautions you should be aware of and the possible side effects for each type of drug used to treat back pain are presented in Table 1. Whatever the drug you are advised to take, it is strongly recommended that you try to use the lowest effective dosage.

Whatever the drug you are advised to take, it is strongly recommended that you try to use the lowest effective dosage.

☐ Spinal Manipulation

This method involves manipulating the spine, ostensibly to realign the joints of the spine, with particular attention given to the condition of the soft tissues of the back and to the level of muscle relaxation. In general, most manipulations are indirectly performed on the pain sufferer. The sufferer's head, shoulders, and hips are twisted by someone in an attempt to realign the spine. Direct manipulation is conducted by applying pressure directly to the spinous processes of specific vertebrae.

Drugs	Purpose	Possible Side Effects	Precautions
Flexeril Norflex Norgesic Parafon Forte Robaxin Roboxisal Soma Valium	Prescription drugs for muscle spasms	Blurred vision Dizziness Drowsiness Increased heart rate Lightheadedness Nausea	Caution should be taken with individuals who have a history of high blood pressure, heart disease, epilepsy, urinary problems, or suicidal tendencies. In addition, these drugs should not be taken along with alcohol, tranquilizers, or anti-depressant drugs.
Butazolidin Clinoril Feldene Indocin Meclomen Motrin Nalfon Naprosyn Tolectin	Prescription anti-inflammatory drugs	Blurred vision, Constipation Cramps, Dizziness Ear problems, Flatulence Fluid retention, Headaches Heartburn, Intestinal bleeding Nausea, Nervousness Ringing in ears, Vomiting	Caution should be taken with individuals who have a history of kidney or liver disease, bleeding problems, or peptic ulcers. In addition, individuals who are physically incapacitated in some way should be particularly cautious.
Advil Aspirin Datril Tylenol	Non-prescription drugs for pain or inflammation	Mild gastrointestinal problems *Nausea, *Cramps *Dizziness, *Headache *Heartburn *Intestinal bleeding *Ringing in ears	Caution should be taken with individuals who have a history of kidney or liver disease or bleeding problems or peptic ulcers.
Codeine Darvon Demerol Percocet Percodan Talwin Tylenol w/Codeine Tylos Vicodin	Prescription drugs for pain	Constipation Depression of breathing Dizziness, Drug addiction Lightheadedness, Nausea Sudden drop in blood pressure, Vomiting	Caution should be taken with individuals who have a history of irregular heartbeats or kidney and liver problems. In addition, individuals who are physically incapacitated in some way should be particularly cautious.

Table 1. Drugs used to treat back pain   (*Note: Effects unlikely with Tylenol or Datril)

The most common practitioners of spinal manipulation are chiropractors. In the United States, chiropractors generally enjoy wide popularity, despite the fact that they are not licensed physicians per se. They cannot prescribe medications or perform surgical operations. Licensed physicians who regularly employ manipulation as a treatment therapy for back pain are known as osteopathic physicians.

With regard to spinal manipulation, two questions arise: "Does it work?" and "What are the dangers attendant to manipulation?"

With regard to spinal manipulation, two questions arise: "Does it work?" and "What are the dangers attendant to manipulation?" The answer to the first question depends almost entirely on whom you ask. Obviously, a lot of positive subjective opinion exists among many of the individuals who have undergone manipulation, or it wouldn't be as popular as it is. On the other hand, argue critics of this technique, there is no statistical evidence to support the claim that spinal manipulation produces a greater reduction in back pain than nature's own healing. In view of the potential dangers, however slight, these individuals conclude that the potential risks of spinal manipulation outweigh the possible gains. The primary risk is the danger that "jostling" the spine, discs, and nerves can result in worsening your condition or cause a far more serious injury. However rare the risks, some individuals would prefer to wait for nature to take its course. Others prefer to try out their options as soon as possible.

Andy Lyons/Getty Images Sport

Back pain, particularly for throwers, is a grim reality

☐ Heat/Cold Therapy

Applying heat or cold to the area of your back that is painful (using an ice pack, heating pad, or lamp) is one of the oldest and most useful methods for relieving muscle spasms. Neither heat nor cold has any curative effects, but each is often successful in relieving muscle spasms. Although heat and cold are opposites, they accomplish the same thing in treating back pain—they increase blood flow to the affected area. Heat involves a reflex mechanism that stimulates the attendant nerves. In turn, the blood vessels in the area to which heat is applied become dilated (expanded) so that more blood flows and the metabolism of the muscles in the area (including the one that is in spasm) is increased. The net result is that the spasm "relaxes."

Applying cold to the area is also effective. Whereas heat expands the blood vessels, cold constricts them. Cold is used following an acute injury to minimize bleeding in an injured area and to minimize swelling. And yet, after cold is used for a period of time, the constricted blood vessels fatigue, and then they relax and dilate. In the end, then, cold and heat have essentially the same effect. Because it is more comfortable, most people prefer heat to cold. In reality, though, cold is uncomfortable only for the first few minutes. Then the area becomes numb. A momentary burning sensation is usually experienced when cold is first applied, but it subsides quickly as the cold therapy is continued.

Two basic questions arise concerning the use of heat or cold as a therapy for treating back pain: "In what form should either be applied?" and "How often should the therapy be used?" Heat can be used in many forms. The simplest, least expensive ones have been found to be as effective as the more expensive methods. At home, you can use a hot water bottle, a heating pad, or a water-heated towel to provide the heat. In general, wet heat has been found to be more successful for most people than dry heat. Wet or dry, you should apply the heat to your muscle spasm for approximately 20-to-30 minutes each session, two-to-four times a day. If you are particularly fortunate or resourceful, a hot tub is often an effective method for relieving a muscle spasm. Physicians will sometimes use deep heat as part of their treatment efforts for your back. Usually, these efforts involve either diathermy or ultrasound. Diathermy uses a machine which, when applied to the area, produces a rapidly alternating electrical field that produces heat below the surface area of your skin by inducing movement in the molecules of your body's tissues. Ultrasound is the deepest form of heat therapy. The ultrasound waves, when applied to your skin where your pain is located, vibrate deep in your tissues, agitating the molecules in the tissues, and in turn causing them to produce heat in the affected area.

Cold is usually applied using an ice pack. Like heat, cold should be used two-to-four times a day. Ice packs should be applied to the affected area for 15-to-20 minutes at a time. A more effective way to use ice for cold therapy is to massage or rub the ice over the affected area. A technique that can be used for doing this is to freeze paper cups three-quarters filled with water. Then simply tear away just enough of the top portion of the cup to expose the ice and gently rub the skin over the affected area with it. Ice should be applied for approximately 30 seconds longer, once the area being rubbed feels numb.

> Neither heat nor cold has any curative effects, but each is often successful in relieving muscle spasms.

□ Massage

Like heat/cold therapy, massage is a method for treating muscle spasms that involves no risks and often provides immediate relief.

Like heat/cold therapy, massage is a method for treating muscle spasms that involves no risks and often provides immediate relief. Massage is passive exercise. Most massage treatments are applied painlessly by having someone rub or knead selected areas of your body. For most individuals, the process has psychological, as well as physiological, benefits. Psychologically, the stroking of our bodies has a soothing effect. Physiologically, massage stimulates the nervous system, which in turn elicits a response by your respiratory and circulatory systems. More blood is brought to the muscle in spasm because the blood vessels are dilated. Nourishment is delivered via the blood to the affected area, and more waste products are removed. The (desired) net result is that massage helps to relax muscles in spasm. Specific types of massage include home (nonprofessional) massage, professional massage, convective tissue massage, and zone therapy. Although none of these forms has any documented curative powers, each seems to be an effective means of relieving back pain for some people.

□ Back-Support Devices

A wide variety of braces, corsets, and collars is currently on the market. Collectively, these devices purport to help relieve back pain by providing abdominal support or by supporting the spine. The better-planned devices are designed for effective abdominal compression and for a slightly flexed lumbar spine. Lumbar flexion minimizes the degree to which the lumbar disc can bulge backwards, and it decreases some of the forces on the lumbar spine's posterior elements.

The question of whether or not these devices actually help has received an equivocal response. Although some back pain sufferers have indicated that the devices did in fact help them, many physicians suggest that wearing these devices might even worsen your condition. If you decide to pursue the use of one of these devices, it is recommended that you proceed cautiously. You should wear one only after having undergone a thorough clinical examination by an experienced physician and a reasonable trial of less expensive therapy.

□ Traction

Traction involves some method for pulling the upper and lower parts of your body in opposite directions to ease your back pain. The machinery used to perform the traction ranges from weights, harnesses, and pulleys to canvas slings (gravity lumbar reduction devices). Proponents of traction claim that it is an effective therapy because it allows you to "stretch" the various elements of the spine, thereby reducing the pressure on the affected nerves. Furthermore, they suggest that traction force can also be directed in a manner that helps to realign the joints of your back into their proper positions. This latter perceived characteristic is closely akin to what is supposed to occur with spinal manipulation. The protocol for applying traction varies from continuously for several hours to intermittent bouts for seconds or minutes. The amount of resistance (pull) typically used for traction for lower back pain ranges from 15 to as much as several hundred pounds. In the case of gravity lumbar-reduction devices, your body's own weight is designed to do the work of the external force.

Considerable debate exists regarding whether or not traction is a useful form of therapy for back pain. Some physicians support its use, whereas others are adamantly against it. Whether to use traction or not is a decision that you should make carefully. Keep in mind that whatever the benefits of traction, they are short-lived. Once you stop being pulled, tugged, and stretched, the elements of your spine will most likely go back to their old positions. One final note: you should religiously avoid all forms of inverted traction (e.g., inversion boots). No particular benefit exists because of your inverted position. On the contrary, an inverted position may cause microscopic bleeding in your eyes or brain.

☐ Exercise

Exercises for back pain are designed to stretch and strength the muscle that support your spine, and to maintain flexibility in those muscles and other supporting structures. If you strengthen certain muscles and stretch certain ligaments, you will be better able to position your back so that the forces affecting your spine are better distributed, the pressure on your facet joints is reduced, and the backward bulging of your discs is minimized. Remember that the strength of your spine can be attributed not to its bones, but to its musculature and the binding (harnessing) effects of its ligaments and connective tissues. There is seemingly wide consensus on the value of exercise to both treat and prevent back pain. Obviously, the primary focus of exercising involves the prevention of back pain. When I was on the faculty at the United States Military Academy at West Point, I developed and successfully tested a system of exercises for stretching and strengthening the lower back. Both research and empirical testing indicated that such a system could be effective in both preventing and treating lower back pain.

☐ Invasive Methods

Invasive methods for treating back pain involve techniques in which your body is invaded (entered) in some way. Acupuncture, trigger point injections, cortisone and novocain injections, and chemonucleolysis are the most common types of invasive methods. Although each of the techniques described in this section have brought relief to some individuals, you should remember that every invasive medical procedure carries some degree of medical risk.

Every invasive medical procedure carries some degree of medical risk.

- *Acupuncture.* Acupuncture has evolved out of three thousand years of Chinese culture and history, and it entails placing thin needles at specific points of your body in order to dull or mask your back pain. The placement of the needles is arranged along lines of energy, called meridians, which run up, down, and around your body, and have purportedly been mapped out over thousands of years by Chinese doctors. In some instances, the needles are supplemented by a low-voltage electrical current. Acupuncture has produced equivocal results. Some individuals swear by its effectiveness, while others claim not to have been helped by the procedure. In support of the former conclusion, some studies have indicated that acupuncture stimulates your body's production of endorphins, thereby relieving your back pain.

- *Trigger-point injections.* Trigger-point treatment involves injecting a local anesthetic into specific points that have been identified as producing pain at other sites in your back. Stimulating the trigger points in your back (unduly sensitive muscle areas) by means of injections is believed to somehow break up the pain cycle in your back. A considerable degree of uncertainty surrounds this method of back treatment. Like acupuncture, the results are mixed—it works well for some, and not at all for others. In addition, in some instances, a simple saline solution or simply needling the trigger point without injecting anything at all has been found to be as successful in treating back pain as an actual injection.

- *Cortisone and novocain injections.* Whereas acupuncture and trigger point injections are basically localized treatments, injecting cortisone and novocain often involves painfully deep injections. Cortisone is injected in hopes of halting local inflammation. Cortisone can also be used for trigger point injections. Novocain is an anesthetic that is injected in an attempt to interrupt the cycle of pain between the local pain and a secondary muscle spasm. In general, cortisone and novocain injections have not been found to be more effective than milder therapies and in some instances have been found to be less effective.

- *Chemonucleolysis.* Chemonucleolysis is a nonsurgical method for treating herniated or bulging discs. It involves injecting an enzyme, chymopapain, into the center portion of an injured disc. The enzyme, once injected, dissolves the nucleus (disc center) only, without affecting the adjacent outer portion of the disc, the nerves, the muscles, and the ligaments. Dissolving the nucleus has been found to reduce the pressure (and thereby the pain) on the nerves near the disc. It should work better for a bulging disc than a herniated disc, where fragments of the disc may be within the spinal canal. The entire procedure for performing chemonucleolysis (from start to finish) takes about an hour and requires approximately one-to-five days of hospitalization afterwards. This therapy has been found to be somewhat safer than surgery, although certainly not risk-free, as very serious allergic reactions to the enzyme have occurred. Its success rate is comparable to other nonsurgical techniques.

☐ Psychological Treatments

Few people realize just how closely their bodies and minds are intertwined. Each of us is, after all, just one organism. Studies have shown that specific psychologically focused therapies can be effective in treating back pain in certain instances. In general, these therapies fall into two groups. The first category involves efforts to relieve tension. If you relieve tension, you decrease the amount of muscular activity. When your muscle is tense, it is contracted. This contraction affects your nerves as well. Tension involves contraction, which in turn results in fatigue and pain because your nerves become electrically irritated. Eventually, you may experience excessive nervous tension, as well as excessive muscular tension. Too much tension can lead to back pain. Controlling your level of tension is essentially a function of learning to relax. It should be noted that relaxation is the opposite of movement. Relaxation is reflected by a reduction or a

Too much tension can lead to back pain.

complete absence of muscular activity in your voluntary muscles. A number of effective techniques for learning how to relax have been developed, including progressive relaxation, mind-to-muscle relaxation, meditation, autogenic training, breathing training, and visualization.

The second group of psychologically focused therapies involves techniques designed to enable you to "control" and "manage" your pain. Somewhat similar to the aforementioned relaxation techniques, these methods also focus on reducing the amount of tension you have. In addition, they attempt to change the way you perceive pain so that you are better prepared to deal with your pain, if necessary. Unfortunately, there are no guarantees that everyone will live a pain-free life. Those who have pain must learn to live with it. Learning how to gain control over your pain and your attendant emotions can be an invaluable action on your part. There are a number of diverse "control-and-manage" pain therapies, including biofeedback, hypnosis, progressive relaxation, visualization, and behavioral analysis.

□ Back Pain Schools/Pain Clinics

A relatively recent development in the search to identify an effective means of treating back pain has been the establishment of organizations known generally as back pain schools or pain clinics. These organizations combine education with treatment within a setting of professional expertise and human understanding. Participation in the programs offered by these groups is designed to allow back pain sufferers to meet each other in a supportive and positive way. The treatment programs in these schools focus on educating you to accept responsibility for caring for your back, training you in the proper techniques for protecting your back, and teaching you how to deal safely with the daily demands of your work and life. By offering the collective expertise of a diverse faculty of specialists and experts on back care, these clinics have been found to be a reasonable, effective, nonsurgical means of treating pain. In many instances, they have proven to be more successful than other nonsurgical methods.

Surgical Therapies

Surgery serves a useful, but limited, function in treating back pain. In the vast majority of cases in which individuals suffer from back pain, surgery is not only unnecessary, but useless. There are only a few times when back surgery is essential. One is when pressure on a nerve must be diminished to relieve unmanageable pain. Another is when progressive nerve damage and paralysis must be halted. A third time is when there is painful motion in the spinal column that must be stopped to prevent recurrence of pain. There are also other, unusual circumstances in which your back pain may not be relieved within a *reasonable* period of time using nonsurgical therapies, and surgery is warranted. Whatever the problem is, though, it should have been present long enough to assume that nature alone is not going to treat it, and, in addition, nonsurgical therapies must have been tried and been unsuccessful. Finally, reasonable evidence should exist that surgery will correct, eliminate, or improve your condition. Although no simple equation exists to give you an answer about whether or not you should have surgery, it is strongly recommended that you adhere to the following advice: "If the risks involved in your surgery are high and the odds it will help are, at least in your opinion, low, it shouldn't be done."

In the vast majority of cases in which individuals suffer from back pain, surgery is not only unnecessary, but useless.

The primary task of your physician, with regard to the question of whether or not you should have surgery, is to ensure that you are given sufficient information to make an informed decision. Cold statistics are one thing; your quality of life is quite another. The better informed you are, the more likely you will make a decision that is appropriate to your situation.

Once you and your physician have reached the decision that surgery is the best course of action for you, the type of surgery performed depends entirely on your condition. These procedures range from laminectomy (disc excision) to salvage back surgery (multiple back operations).

☐ Laminectomy

The most common surgical procedure for back pain is a laminectomy.

The most common surgical procedure for back pain is a laminectomy. A laminectomy involves making a small opening in the lamina (the bone that is part of the vertebra that covers the affected level of the spinal canal). Once your physician can get at the slipped or herniated disc material that is pressing on the nerve root, it is removed. Any loose fragments within the space between the vertebrae or within the disc are also removed to prevent the possibility of the recurrence of pain. The operation, conducted with the patient under full anesthesia, normally takes anywhere from 30-to-90 minutes in the average-sized individual. Following surgery, the hospitalization period usually lasts from three-to-four days. After your discharge from the hospital, you should be able to resume full-time work in approximately three-to-four weeks. Full recovery (the operation is fully forgotten) usually takes about six months. The success rate for this type of surgical therapy is often as high as 90 percent.

☐ Spinal Fusion

Spinal fusion, a special type of back surgery, is an operation in which bone from somewhere else in your body, or from a donor's body, is grafted onto living bone in your back. Eventually, the grafted bone in your body will be replaced by living bone produced by your body. In the meantime, you have made a strong, stable union between two or more vertebrae (the bones selected for fusion). This stable union obviously reduces the motion at that particular segment of your spine. Any pain that had previously been produced or irritated by the excessive motion that existed will subside. The success rate of spinal fusion operations has not been found to be above the host of nonsurgical therapies discussed previously. For that reason, the incidence of spinal fusions has decreased dramatically in recent years. Except in instances in which the likely benefits of spinal fusion are well-documented (e.g., following a severe spinal fracture in which the joints between the vertebrae are so severely injured that the stability of your spine is in question), the possible negative complications from a spinal fusion are too extensive to warrant such an operation.

☐ Surgery to Relieve Spinal Stenosis

Spinal stenosis is a condition in which the space in your spinal canal is not big enough. This condition can be congenital. More often, though, it is the result of arthritis and bone spurs in your vertebral bodies or facet joints that cause narrowing of the spinal canal. Stenosis can also be caused by a degenerative or herniated disc. The surgical procedure for this condition involves removing any and all structures that are impinging on the nerves within the spinal canal. If the need for this operation is confirmed beforehand by radiographic studies (myelogram or a CAT scan), the operation is usually successful.

☐ Surgery to Treat Infections

Infections of the spine can be quite painful. Although antibiotics alone can often eliminate such infections, in some instances surgery may be necessary to treat them. In these cases surgery is performed to drain the infection and to remove enough of the soft tissue and bone to cure the infection, while maintaining as much of the spine as possible. A thorough cleansing of the area with a sterile solution containing antibiotics is also done to prevent recurrence of the infection. In some cases, depending upon how much of the bone had to be removed, a bone graft may subsequently be required to fuse and reconstruct the spine.

☐ Surgery to Remove Tumors

The decision on whether or not to surgically remove a tumor must be made taking several factors into account. Can it be treated with chemotherapy or radiation? Is it benign or malignant? Did it originate in your spine, or has it migrated from elsewhere in your body? What are the risks involved in surgery for this specific tumor? What are the probable outcomes of both performing and not performing this surgery? In general, the procedures of this type of surgery are similar to those for surgery to treat infections. Because the surgeon has to eliminate the entire tumor *plus* an appropriate margin of normal spine adjacent to the tumor, the surgical risks and skills needed to perform the operation successfully are substantially higher when operating to remove a tumor than for treating a spinal infection. The likelihood of needing a bone graft or other type of spinal replacement device or material to rebuild the spine after this operation is also increased.

☐ Surgery to Treat Injuries

Moderate fractures of your spine tend to heal without severe pain. Surgery for spinal fractures depends to some extent on whether the fracture is old or recent. An old fracture probably will not require surgery unless severe pain is present and the pain can be reasonably attributed to the fracture. In this instance, your physician would probably immobilize you in a brace or body cast. If your pain decreases, a spinal fusion operation would probably help. Whether or not surgery would be required for a recent fracture depends on the extent of any vertebrae damage. If your vertebrae were extensively damaged, especially in your lower spine, you probably would undergo an operation in which stainless steel rods would be implanted next to your spine. Attached to your normal spine above and below your injury, these rods would help hold your spine in place while it heals. On the other hand, injuries such as mild compression fractures, especially in the more stable area of the spine like the thoracic vertebrae, may require no more treatment than restricting the movement of the affected area while your fracture heals.

Whether or not surgery would be required for a recent fracture depends on the extent of any vertebrae damage.

☐ Surgery to Interrupt Your Nervous System

There are three surgical procedures designed to interrupt your nervous system. In each, an operation is performed to "inhibit" your pain by surgically cutting a specific pain pathway. The rationale is that the sensation of pain cannot be transmitted to your brain if the pain pathway has been severed. In a procedure called a *tractotomy*, a localized segment of your spinal thalamic tract is cut at the site where the sensory part of the affected nerves from your back and limbs enter your spinal cord. In a procedure called a rhizotomy, the nerves around the affected intervertebral joints are destroyed in an attempt to "deaden" the pain perceived to be emanating from these joints. Neither a tractotomy nor a rhizotomy has been found to be particularly successful. As a result, these procedures rarely are performed nowadays. In a procedure called a cordotomy, the pain pathways in the upper thoracic or cervical spinal cord are severed. This operation is only performed when a terminally ill cancer patient has severe, localized pain in one area of the body (such as one leg) and has a limited life expectancy.

☐ Salvage Back Surgery

Salvage back surgery is performed on someone who has already had two or more operations for back pain. Numerous studies suggest that additional surgical operations often have decreasing chances of success. As a result, except in those extremely rare circumstances when multiple back operations are warranted, you should be very cautious before undergoing surgery again.

As a throws coach, dealing with back pain in your athletes is a grim reality.

The Next Step

As a throws coach, dealing with back pain in your athletes is a grim reality. Just as real is the fact that the load forces that your athletes place on their bodies while performing their event exposes them to likelihood of incurring this painful, debilitating condition. Although no foolproof plan exists for preventing back pain, you can adopt a thoughtful, systematic strategy for minimizing the risk of your athletes suffering back pain. At the heart of this strategy should be an effort to strengthen the extensor muscles in their lower back and to maintain the flexibility level in their hamstring muscles.

28

Plyometric Training for Track and Field

By Tom Pukstys, CSCS

In order to maximize the human body's potential for athletic performance, training must involve a balanced attack on strength, power, and speed. Using a pyramid as a model, the base area represents strength, the middle represents power and speed, and the peak represents peak performance in all categories combined. When an athlete trains, he must address all areas to reach his potential.

One of the most efficient and effective methods for gaining power and speed is plyometric training. Plyometric training can be defined as doing any athletic motion quickly or explosively, and also repetitively. Most coaches understand plyometrics as dealing with the legs, but the upper body can perform plyometric movements also. Plyometric training can offer an athlete the final piece in training to reach his peak performance due to the intensity and speed gained from the movements.

> Most coaches understand plyometrics as dealing with the legs, but the upper body can perform plyometric movements also.

Plyometric Training for Track and Field Athletes

Each event in track and field has different needs, but plyometric training can be used universally for all track and field athletes and be effective for everybody. Most plyometric exercises are jumping-based. Some plyometric exercises also involve throwing something, such as a medicine ball. Among the issues involving plyometric exercises, two of the most important areas of consideration are safety and how much exercise to do.

☐ *Safety.* Because jumping and throwing can be aggressive and explosive in nature, there is a degree of danger involved. In this regard, the following guidelines are applicable:

• Always weigh the risk and the reward. Pushing dangerous limits doesn't bring better results.

- Flooring or surface used: The most important aspect for injury prevention can be the floor used for jump training. Grass is best, or use softer floors indoors.

- Never jump down stairs, but up the stairs is acceptable.

- If throwing medicine balls, allow for a strong wall, with no glass or windows nearby.

☐ *How much to do?*

- Since exploding physically places more demands on the nervous system of your body, rest plays an important role. It takes an extra day, compared to general muscular training, to recover from hard plyometric training.

- Usually 50-to-100 jump contacts are an appropriate amount for a plyometric-exercise session.

- Exercising every other day is great, but lower-impact training is possible on a daily basis.

- Perform less plyometric-exercise training during the season; short and fast explosive training will be enough.

- Use low-impact plyometrics to build a fitness base.

- If an athlete fails to execute a jump because he is exhausted, that individual has done too much plyometric-exercise training.

If an athlete fails to execute a jump because he is exhausted, that individual has done too much plyometric-exercise training.

Choosing an Exercise

Use common sense and try to relate to the athlete's needs. Jumpers can perform both one- and two-leg jumps. Sprinters use higher speed single-leg bounds. Throwers need both upper- and lower-body exercises. Sample exercises include single-leg patterns, two-leg patterns, upper-body patterns, and patterns for the whole team together—mini circuits for fitness and power.

☐ Single-leg exercises:

- *Single-leg box jumps.* Stand with one leg on a box or stair, jump up, switch legs in the air, and repeat. A box or stair of 16 inches is enough for even the tallest athletes, and 20 repetitions or less is standard.

- *Single-leg bounds.* Simple repetitive bounding on one leg. Use a soft surface if possible, and go for maximum distance. Three or four sets of 10 jumps are standard.

- *Standing-triple jump.* Start on two legs, and bound onto one leg, then the other, and land into a sand pit, or on a soft pad. This can be measured for distance to monitor improvement. Performing 10-to-20 repetitions a workout are enough.

☐ Two-leg exercises:

- *Standing double-bound.* Two jumps in a row with two legs. This can be measured if you jump into sand. You can also use a hurdle or pad to challenge the athlete to reach for greater power on the second jump. 10-to-20 repetitions a session are standard.

- *Box jumps.* On and off a box with two legs. Maximum height will be about 32 inches for high-level athletes, when most will be fine at 20 inches. Five sets of 10 are standard.

- *Bounding up stairs.* The reliable method of bounding up bleachers has been and will continue to be a solid way to improve power and fitness in athletes. Because it is possible to vary the intensity by skipping stairs, the volume of training in this instance depends on the intensity level of the training.

☐ Upper-body exercises:

- *Bench press-style pushes.* With an athlete who is lying on his back, another athlete drops a medicine ball onto the outreached hands of the athlete who is on his back. The ball should be caught and released as fast as possible. Throw it as high as you can. Three-to-five sets of 10 repetitions with medicine balls weighing six-to-12 pounds are standard.

- *Chest pass.* While standing, simply throw the ball with two arms as hard as possible at a wall and repeat for 10 repetitions. Three-to-five sets are standard.

- *Plyometric push-ups.* With one arm on a medicine ball in push-up position, the athlete must explode enough to switch the ball to the other hand before completing the next push-up.

The reliable method of bounding up bleachers has been and will continue to be a solid way to improve power and fitness in athletes.

Tim DeFrisco/Getty Images Sport

In order to maximize the human body's potential for athletic performance, training must involve a balanced attack on strength, power, and speed.

☐ Team training and conditioning. Circuit training is ideal for groups, circumstances in which both volume and intensity of exercise can be manipulated to a point where exceptional results in fitness training can be achieved for all athletes on the team. An example of timed circuits would be to use 20 seconds of training, followed by 20 seconds of rest, with several exercises, for example:

- *Depth jumps.* Touching the ground and leaping as high as possible.

- *Leg-switch jumps.* Start with a lunge, jump up, and switch leg positions.

- *Calf jumps.* Use straight legs, and focus on a calf-oriented jump.

29

Three Ways to Train for Strength

By Robb Rogers, M.Ed., CSCS

There are only three ways to train for strength. You can add load (resistance), add reps (volume), or add speed to the movement. This article explains how to do all three within one training session, using one exercise. Generally, this type of training is utilized when performing big lifts that involve many large muscle groups. These lifts are the core or traditional power lifts (e.g., bench, squat, and deadlift).

Adding load to the lift is a very traditional way to strength train. After each set, weight is added to the bar in order to increase the resistance. As the sets pile up, so does the weight. The reps will stay the same or go down as the load increases. For example:

Adding load to the lift is a very traditional way to strength train.

A			B		
Reps		Load	Reps		Load
10	@	50%	10	@	50%
8	@	60%	5	@	60%
6	@	70%	5	@	70%
4	@	80%	5	@	80%
3	@	85%	5	@	80%
2	@	90%	5	@	80%
Total reps 33			Total reps 33		
Average load 72.14%			Average load 70%		

A second way to gain strength is to add reps or sets to the training program. This step increases the amount of overall work done in the training session. For example:

	A			B	
Reps		Load	Reps		Load
10	@	50%	10	@	50%
8	@	60%	5	@	60%
6	@	70%	5	@	70%
4	@	80%	5	@	80%
3	@	85%	5	@	80%
2	@	90%	5	@	80%
10	@	70%	5	@	80%
5	@	80%			
Total reps 43			Total reps 45		
Average load 72.14%			Average load 72.5%		

Another way to train for strength is to add speed to the movement.

The third way to train for strength is to add speed to the movement. In this instance, the bar is moved as fast as possible through the concentric (up) phase of the motion, regardless of the load involved. The bar may not look as if it is moving fast or even faster than normal, but the athlete is attempting to move it as quickly as possible. The workout stays the same in quantitative terms of sets, reps, and load, but the quality of effort is much greater, as is the effect of training.

Andy Lyons/Getty Images Sport

There are only three ways to train for strength.

Is it possible to do all three of these training techniques within the same exercise? Absolutely! The key is to do as few repetitions as possible as you warm up to the movement and work up to the heavier loads. As soon as you get up to the "work-load zone," then start to train with "speed." At the end of the workout, do a burnout set with the same load you used when you trained with quick and heavy. At this point, if you need to cheat on the burnout set, cheat and take the muscles past the point of no return. Just remember to have great spotters and good technique. The following example illustrates such an approach:

The key is to do as few repetitions as possible as you warm up to the movement and work up to the heavier loads.

	Example A			**Example B**			
Speed	Zones Reps	Load	Speed	Reps	Load	Speed	
	5	@	55%	moderate		5 @	55%
moderate							
warm-up	5 @	65%	moderate	4 @	65%	moderate	
	5 @	75%	moderate	3 @	75%	moderate	
				3 @	80%	moderate	
workload	5x5 80% @		as fast as possible	8x3 @	85%	as fast as possible	
burnout	10@	80%	cheat if necessary	6 @	85%	cheat if necessary	
Total reps 50				Total Reps 45			
Average Load 75%				Average Load 80%			

As your training progresses and the quality of your efforts are better, you will be able to move up on the training scale. In other words, you will be able to go heavier, longer, and move weight faster during the workout for better effort quality. This approach will create a better quality of training and, in turn, a stronger you.

30

Organizing the Training of Hammer Throwers

By Mohamad Saatara

The goal for this article is to provide an outline and methodology for the training of hammer throwers. As with any endeavor, precise planning, organization, and goal setting are the hallmarks of success. The initial step in coaching the hammer throw is to devise an overall technical model, which can then be taught to athletes. The athlete's physical and psychological characteristics must be considered, because they will have an extensive influence on the athlete's execution of movement and performance.

Initially, a long-term plan and an outline of training goals should be devised. It is important to note that long-term training plans do not have to be specific; they are used as an overall guide for progression. Testing methods can be successfully utilized to monitor the progress of the thrower. Testing can also be used to motivate the thrower during periods when there are no competitions or when the thrower is still not ready to compete.

> Testing can also be used to motivate the thrower during periods when there are no competitions or when the thrower is still not ready to compete.

General Technical Model

There is extensive material available in the literature regarding hammer throw technique. The following is an overview of the most important technical aspects of the hammer throw. For discussion purposes, the hammer throw is divided into three general segments: initial swings and entry, the turns, and the final delivery. Furthermore, the turns can also be divided into two parts: the double-support phase (defined as when both feet are on the ground), and the single-support phase (when only one foot is on the ground). It is very important to emphasize that the throw is a seamless movement, from the initial swing to the final delivery. Many technical and developmental problems can be avoided if this factor is reinforced early on in an athlete's training. The hallmarks of efficient technique are proportionally long double-support phases, during which the thrower can accelerate the implement, an athletic and stable posture through which the thrower can move quickly, and maximized turning radius of the hammer. Several main points should be observed as an athlete throws:

☐ *Posture and initial entry.* The thrower must maintain a posture where the center of gravity is kept over the feet. The head is kept in a neutral position, while the shoulders, upper back, and arms are relaxed. The knees and ankles maintain a comfortable flexed or bent position. The degree of bending of the knees is dependent on experience, personal preference, and general strength levels. The posture in the initial swings and entry is of the utmost importance because the movements of the entry dictate the movement of the athlete through the consecutive turns and delivery. The turning action is initiated by the musculature of the feet, legs, and torso.

☐ *Effective radius and acceleration of the hammer.* The hammer should be kept as far away from the athlete as possible, while maintaining proper posture. During the initial swings, the hammer is kept on the right side of the body. The low point of the hammer is kept to the right of the athlete until entry into the first turn, when the low point is moved in front of the athlete and is left there for the duration of the throw. The implement maintains a long circular or semi-ovoid path through the turns. The hammer is accelerated at the initiation of each double-support phase, with a pushing action of the right side of the body. At no time should the hammer be accelerated by a "pulling" or "dragging" action by the musculature of the left side of the body, since this will lead to the reduction of an effective radius and also lead to a breaking action during the turns, along with a host of other detrimental effects. The athlete must not interfere with the position of the low and high point of the hammer during the throw. The thrower should not "counter" or pull the hammer into the turns and the release, because doing so will cause a marked change in the path of the hammer and disrupt balance.

The athlete must not interfere with the position of the low and high point of the hammer during the throw.

☐ *Movement of the feet.* The feet should move through the throw with precise and deliberate action. The pivoting action of the feet should be performed with the mass of the athlete placed directly over the feet. The axis of rotation should be maintained near or over the left foot, which allows the right side to be free to be moved violently from turn to turn. The feet should move through the throw in conjunction with the hammer or slightly earlier.

The precise pivoting action of the left foot must be emphasized. The turns are initiated by a pivoting and driving action of the right foot, followed by the pivoting of the left heel. The right foot can be placed either on the heel, flat, or ball of the foot. The pivoting action of the right foot should always conclude with a deliberate and forceful drive from the ball of the foot.

☐ *Rhythmic movement through the throw.* There should be a deliberate increase in the velocity of the hammer through the throw, with maximum velocity achieved at the point of release. This increase in speed should be dictated by the movement of the feet and lower body. In each turn, the thrower must strive for longer double-support phases. The athlete must never try to "force" the hammer with the upper body, because this will disrupt the rhythmic character of the throw. The thrower must remain relaxed through the release of the hammer. The throw is concluded with a forceful movement of the feet. The release should feel relaxed, fast, and athletic.

Developing Training Plans

Organizing the training of hammer throwers must follow a long- and short-term plan. Zaitchouk, Bundarchuk, and Verkhoshansky, along with others, have described detailed methods of developing long- and short-term training plans for the hammer throw. Constructing a training plan for the hammer throw can follow classic periodization models, or be divided into blocks of specific work.

Training for hammer throwers should be geared toward developing specific power and technical proficiency.

Training for hammer throwers should be geared toward developing specific power and technical proficiency. It is of the utmost importance to develop the movement patterns associated with high-velocity activities as early in training as possible. This urgency is due to the way the nervous system learns and organizes movement. Movement is not only organized by the pattern of muscular recruitment, but also by how fast muscles are recruited and used.

Initially, the mechanical and rhythmic characteristics of a throw should be emphasized. Walking with one or two hammers, drills for footwork, and performing throws from multiple turns (four-to-10 turns) are excellent ways of developing these aspects of the throw. These exercises should always be concluded with a relatively fast release. Technical proficiency at high velocities can be accomplished by initially using lighter hammers, or competition weight hammers on shorter (10cm-to-15cm from competition-length) wires. Once the athlete has developed the requisite technical proficiency event, specific strength and power can be developed by using kettle bells, puds, and heavier hammers (men: 8kg up to 12kg; women: 5kg up to 8kg) with regular and short wires.

The initial step in devising a training plan is to measure the athlete's physical abilities to provide a baseline of the thrower's technical and physical characteristics. The Test Quadathlon, vertical jump test, and other tests to measure the athlete's ability for power output are very useful. The thrower's event-specific abilities can be observed by how fast and how accurately he can perform turns, with and without implements, and how efficiently the thrower delivers the hammer or a kettle bell from preliminary swings, one, two, and three turns. The coach should also inquire about the thrower's own performance goals for the short and long term. An analysis of the previous year's performances also provides great insight into the thrower's abilities. Testing and evaluation of the athlete should also be performed at regular intervals throughout the training periods to provide feedback on the effectiveness of training.

Once a fair understanding exists of the thrower's abilities and the thrower's desired performance, a long-term training plan with a set of goals can be constructed. Annual or biannual training plans seem to be the most manageable. Training for hammer throwers, therefore, can be divided into four general areas:

☐ *Throwing of the hammer.* Throwing light, medium, and heavy hammers with various length wires, throwing the hammer from multiple turns, and throwing at different intensities.

❑ *Event-specific exercises.* Turning drills with hammers and throwing of medicine balls, shots, puds, and kettle bells with one or two hands.

❑ *General athletic exercises.* Sprints and plyometrics (performed in a linear and twisting manner), running, coordination exercises, and gymnastic exercises.

❑ *Strength and resistance exercises.* Classic weightlifting exercises (e.g., pulls, cleans, snatches, squats, presses, etc.), twisting exercises with weight plates, dumbbells, and bars, and bodybuilding and joint rehabilitation exercises.

Training section	Duration	General goals	Throwing	Special exercises	Fitness and mobility	Resistance training
Initial conditioning	4-6 weeks	Regaining general abilities and balance	Throwing from multiple turns and drill using competition weight hammers	High volume throws with lighter medicine balls and light shots	Coordination and sprinting exercises, low intensity, and high-volume jumps	General strength exercises (squats, presses), circuit training
Technical development	6-8 weeks	Mastering and developing technical model at high velocities. Continuing strength and athletic abilities	Some throwing from multiple turns, throws with lighter implements, and competition hammers with short wires	Medium volume throws with medicine balls. Throws with lighter kettle bells	Sprinting, moderate intensity plyometric exercises, bounding, and jumping	General strength exercises and Olympic lifts for "base strength." Some circuit training, and light twisting exercises
General power	8 weeks	Developing maximum general power and specific strength	Throws with heavier hammers and competition hammers, along with short heavy hammers and puds from 1, 2, and 3 turns. Throws with moderate intensity	Heavy medicine ball throws, throwing exercises with puds, kettle bells from 1, 2, and 3 turns	High-intensity jumping and plyometric exercises, focus on single jumps. Short sprints	General strength exercises and Olympic lifts focused on developing maximum strength. Moderate twisting exercises
Specific Power I	4 weeks	Developing event-specific power. Focus on developing special exercises for event-specific strength	Throws with short and heavy hammers, throws focused on developing maximum release velocity from 1, 2, and 3 turns	High proportion of training volume focused on pud and kettle bell exercises and shot throws	Bounding and multiple jumps with high intensity. Running with resistance (on hills, or with weighted vests)	General strength exercises with emphasis on explosive movement, along with twisting exercises
Competition (Indoor)	4 weeks	This is a continuation of the specific-power phase with some indoor competitions	Same as above, some throws with indoor weight once or twice per week. Throws with high intensity	Same as above	Same as above	Focus on the Olympic lifts and rhythmic execution of these lifts from hanging position. Heavy twisting exercises
Specific Power II	8 weeks	Developing event-specific power with emphasis on velocity of movement and final velocity at release	Reduced volume of throws with short and heavy hammers, introduction of lighter hammers. Throws for moderate intensity, some high-intensity sessions	High-intensity kettle bell and pud exercises and throws. Throwing of heavy medicine balls	Bounding and multiple jumping exercises along with jumps performed with twisting movements	General strength exercise with emphasis on explosive movement. Olympic lifts performed from hanging position and rhythmic execution. Twisting exercises with emphasis on speed of movement
Competition (Outdoor)	8-14 weeks	Preparing for competitions	Throws performed with light and competition-weight hammers. Few throws with short, heavy hammers. Emphasis on competition preparation	Shot throws, kettle bell, and pud exercises with emphasis on final velocity	High-intensity rhythmic jumps, and plyometrics very low volume	Maintenance of power levels. Olympic lifts for rhythm with very fast movements
Rest period	4 weeks	Rest and recovery from training	Few throws or rest	None	Some distance running or easy jogging	Maintenance exercises

During the early phases of training, throwing of the hammers (especially lighter hammers) and general athletic exercises should dominate the total volume of training. Maximal strength and power training, along with event-specific exercises, should be mostly used before the competition phase and during the early competitive period. During the competitive period, the focus should shift to maximizing event-specific power by using event-specific exercises, with an emphasis on maximum release velocity, multiple jumps (three-to-five jumps per set), and performing rhythmic weightlifting exercises (e.g., three-to-four pulls with a barbell, concluded with a clean or snatch). The chart on page 145 illustrates an example of a training plan for a moderately trained male hammer thrower.

The pattern of development for this particular training plan initially focuses on technical execution, followed by incremental development of general strength, general power, specific strength, and, finally, execution of the throw at competitive levels. It is important to note that the throwing of the hammer should be the central focus of training, with the other training exercises used to first extend general athletic abilities, and then to develop maximum strength, and, finally, power.

Mike Hewitt/Getty Images Sport

Maximal strength and power training, along with event-specific exercises, should be mostly used before the competition phase and during the early competitive period.

Conclusion

The coach or trainer should have an excellent understanding of the technical model that will be used for throwing the hammer. As the old adage goes, "many roads lead to Rome." The coach must be open-minded in his or her approach to teaching and training for the hammer throw and use methods and teaching guides that best fit the athlete's cognitive, physical, and technical abilities. It is of vital importance for the development of hammer throwers that they should initially have an excellent "athletic" base. This factor refers to the fact that the thrower should have the ability to move his body and generate power in three dimensions. As training continues, the coach should also encourage the hammer thrower to build the skills needed to cope with competitive situations and the stresses involved with competition.

It is of vital importance for the development of hammer throwers that they should initially have an excellent "athletic" base.

Selected Hammer Throwing References

Bartonietz, K., Barklay, L., and Bathercole, D. (1997). Characteristics of Top Performances in the Women's Hammer Throw: Basics and Techniques of the World's Best Athletes. *New Studies in Athletics*, 12:2-3; 101-109.

Bartonietz, K. and Larsen B. (1997). General and Event Specific Considerations in Peaking for the Main Competition. *New Studies in Athletics*, 12: 2-3, 75-86.

Pedemonte, J. (1985). Hammer. In *Athletes in Action*, Howard Payne (Ed), Pelham books, 237-262.

Petrov, V. (1985). Hammer Throw Technique and Drills. In *The Throws*, Jesse Jarver (Ed.), Tafnews Press, 127-130.

Reidel, B. (2002 translation). The Transition is of Vital Importance! *Leichtathletiktraining*, 13 (10 and 11).

Verkhoshansky, Y.V. (1988). *Programming and Organization of Training.* Sportivny Press.

31
Right-Sided Hammer Technique

By Al Schoterman

A very high level of fitness, specific strength and speed must be achieved for throwing the hammer 80 meters and above that distance.

This article is a combination of many past ideas, methods, and old vocabulary, mixed with modern technology. The result is a common explanation of high-speed, long-distance throwing. I personally have been involved with the hammer throw for the past forty years. Never having seen or experienced the hammer before I ended up throwing it 231 feet and .5 inches after a mere three years of practice, resulting in a NCAA record. I then had the pleasure of coaching Jud Logan at Kent State University. Jud is now an excellent physical fitness, conditioning, and weight-training coach for all throws. Jud can be contacted at Ashland College in Ohio where he serves as the head coach of the track team. A very high level of fitness, specific strength and speed must be achieved for throwing the hammer 80 meters and above that distance. The farther the athlete throws past 80 meters, "active rest," numbers of and intensity involving synapse nerve firings in training, and pre-meet preparation become very important. This technique is very high powered and dynamic, using all available laws of physics dynamics to accelerate the hammer head. First some old and new analogies on concept vocabulary.

Old	New
Left-sided throw	Right-side drive
Lift off of right left—long duration	Lift off of right left—short duration
Stay upright and extend shoulders	Bend from waist – extend shoulders
Lift ball at release	Plant, lift head back, and sling ball
Sit in middle off wind	Wind on right side
Turn faster = throw farther	Wind faster = throw farther
Tug of war	Tension on wire
Accelerate ball 140-170 degrees	Accelerate ball 340 degrees

The throw will be divided into the (1) wind and the entry, (2) lift off and landing, (3) landing to zero degrees, and (4) delivery.

Wind and Entry

A normal or a pendulum wind can be used. I prefer the pendulum, because as it starts to use the ball's potential energy, which will be later transferred into the speed of the hammer head. Either way, the thrower MUST literally stand on an almost straight right leg, (90 per cent of his weight on his right leg). Using the pendulum wind, the second wind descends (drops) to a fairly flat plane. The thrower must bend from the waist, extending the shoulders out. When properly done, the ball will "snap" along with the wire as the hammer starts to accelerate. You are now countering the ball with the biggest part of the body, your backside (gluteus maximus). Make no mistake, you cannot beat the ball's force, but you CAN control it to your advantage creating maximum tension on the wire. The ball and thrower are now in harmony and create a "unit" that doesn't change much throughout the remainder of the throw.

> You cannot beat the ball's force, but you CAN control it to your advantage creating maximum tension on the wire.

Lift Off and Landing

Lift off occurs at about 90 to 120 degrees. The ball decelerates when one leg is removed from the ground. Consequently, the less time the leg is airborne, the better. Because the thrower is right-sided for a longer period of time, the lower left leg is on a backward angle, allowing the right leg to lift off and take a "short cut" and land, immediately. When the right leg lands, the athlete has reassured the right-leg position to again use the backside for countering the velocity of the ball.

Landing to 0 Degrees (Start Position or End of the First Turn)

After landing, the thrower is still right-sided. The thrower and the ball collectively travel to 0 degrees. At this point, the hammer is massively accelerated on completion of turns 1 and 2 for three turners, and for 1, 2, and 3 for four turners, all at just before 0 degrees. The thrower will slightly straighten his legs as the ball passes 0 degrees. The thrower goes up as the ball pulls down, creating huge wire tension. Hence, tremendous hammer head speed is caused. This movement occurs naturally if the body is right-sided and all other components are correct. I truly believe this movement cannot be taught, as it must be felt. When all is correctly aligned, the momentum added to the wire is enormous and transferred to the hammer head. The thrower must have his legs straightening against the ball at 0 degrees to reach far distances or better throws at reduced strength and developmental levels.

Delivery

The delivery is a lot different than that of the old technique. It is actually a continuation of the actual throw. The athlete lifts off, plants the right leg, starts to block with the head, straightens the back, and "slings" the ball. The thrower never really lifts the ball as was the usual practice with the old technique.

Summary of Major Points:

1. The hammer head accelerates for almost 360 degrees.

2. Turning speed is NOT directly proportional to hammer head speed. You can turn fast without increasing great distance.

3. The right leg and foot are the slowest turning speed of the "unit."

4. Counter and radius are being worked constantly, but counter dominates left side; radius dominates right side.

5. A thrower lands, and the radius extends dramatically.

6. By being completely right-sided, the radius-and-counter combination creates hammer-wire tension, leading to constantly accelerating hammer head speed.

7. The thrower and ball link up off the wind and form a unit that self-generates speed, which is difficult to slow down.

8. As a comparison to a planetary system of circular moving objects, this is the order of what turns speed-wise, from fastest to slowest: hammer head, hands, shoulders, left leg, hips, right leg.

Mike Hewitt/Getty Images Sport

32

Balancing Workouts in Training the Collegiate and Post-Collegiate Hammer Thrower*

By Paul E. Turner, Ph.D.

As coaches, we face many constraints in providing good training programs to our charges. At the collegiate level, many of these restrictions are the result of NCAA rules, such as mandatory days off, hourly time restrictions, and a limited number of practice opportunities. As we work with post-collegiate athletes, we encounter different types of restrictions, including the use of the university's facilities, the athlete's work schedule (unless they are fortunate enough to have either a stipend or are making enough money through athletics to support themselves—and everyone knows how rare that is for a thrower), meeting schedules (athletes often have weeks at a time with no meets and then a flurry of competitions), and the schedule of the coach. Because of these limitations, it is very important for the coach to be able to provide a well-balanced training program that is, by nature, a compromise (who wouldn't want to be able to spend more time training?), but one that is sufficient to allow development.

> It is very important for the coach to be able to provide a well-balanced training program that is, by nature, a compromise, but one that is sufficient to allow development.

The first step in implementing a balanced training program is to ascertain the components of such a program. A balanced training program consists of several dimensions. Actual throwing, technical development via drills, strength training, general conditioning, specific conditioning through plyometrics and medicine ball workouts, and proper recovery are all important to a balanced program. Different phases of the annual training cycle require a different balance of these essential activities and therein lies the issue at hand— implementing the proper balance throughout the year. It is of paramount importance that the coach be able to identify what training aspects are most important for each athlete. While it is easy to have a generic workout program that applies to all athletes, it is also wrong to do so. Likewise, it would also be possible to quantify a microcycle quite easily (number of repetitions in the weight room, number of throws per week, duration of sprints and recovery, volume of plyometrics, number of drills, number of medicine ball throws/exercises, etc.) and settle for applying this blindly to a group of athletes. However, it must never be forgotten that there are individual differences to be considered. There may be five different programs in place for five different throwers. Workouts can and should vary according to the demands of the athlete and the situation. Workouts are written in ink, not carved in stone.

While it is easy to have a generic workout program that applies to all athletes, it is also wrong to do so.

Following the identification of the necessary components, the next consideration in establishing a balanced training regimen is to determine whether the training will be based upon a mono-cycle (hammer only) or a bi-cycle (weight throw indoors and hammer outdoors). This step will greatly influence the type and duration of activities at any given point in the program. The coach and athlete will establish a priority the week in which they desire to be at their physical and technical peak (e.g., conference championship, NCAAs, USATF Championships, etc.) and work backward from that point to establish the competition and preparatory phases of the program. There will be competition and preparatory phases for the mono-cycle and two of each of these phases for a bi-cycle (that is, the athlete will have to be prepared to throw the weight well in late February/early March and then be able to throw the hammer well in June/July). The bi-cycle obviously poses issues in an annual program because it is always better to have a longer uninterrupted preparatory phase in order to maximize our training base, but this cannot be avoided in some circumstances (most prevalent for the collegiate athlete who is expected to provide team points at the indoor conference meet).

The Mono-Cycle

It is often impossible to accurately rank order the importance of the type of activity during the preparatory phase. For example, a rank order of activities during September through October may be:

1. Strength training—anatomical adaptation
2. General conditioning—running and stadium work
3. Throwing
4. Drills
5. Plyometrics
6. Medicine ball

In theory, the amount of time spent on each of these activities should be congruent with their rank order. However, due to environmental considerations (it starts getting dark and cold earlier in New England than it does in the Southwest), it may be necessary to spend more time throwing during this time, before the athlete has to move indoors and begin emphasizing drills to a greater extent. Therefore, while the rank order importance may not change, the amount of time spent in any given area may shift. While it cannot be denied that the primary focus of the early preparatory phase is just that, preparation for the long season ahead, consideration must be given to other demands. A hypothetical breakdown and time per week (based upon a daily four-hour training block, five days per week) are as follows:

1.	Strength training	30%	6 hours
2.	General conditioning	20%	4 hours
3.	Throwing	20%	4 hours
4.	Drills	15%	3 hours
5.	Plyometrics	8%	1.6 hours
6.	Medicine ball	7%	1.4 hours

There are numerous workouts that cross over from one category to another. For example, during the preparatory phase, a plyometrics circuit routine involving a high volume of low-impact exercises with minimal recovery provides both general conditioning and plyometric benefits. These numbers may be quite adequate and accurate for an athlete training at the U.S. Olympic Training Center in California, but might otherwise be insufficient and incorrect for someone who is training in Wisconsin. For that individual, the following schedule might be a better advised option:

1.	Strength training	28%	5.6 hours
2.	General conditioning	15%	3 hours
3.	Throwing	27%	5.4 hours
4.	Drills	15%	3 hours
5.	Plyometrics	8%	1.6 hours
6.	Medicine ball	7%	1.4 hours

In any given week during this phase, the percentages will change. Even more specifically, these percentages will vary from day to day. Not all of these activities can be done each day. The coach must balance the workouts from day to day and from week to week. Also, factors such as an increase in throwing volume resulting in less time devoted to drills must be considered. A rainy day can also throw a wrench into a rigid plan. The coach and the athlete must be flexible. Outside stressors can influence the direction of any given practice. A hard day at work or a student not getting any sleep due to "pulling an all-nighter" will dictate what is prescribed for a particular session. The coach must not forget that the stress of daily routines (uncontrollable by the coach) will be added to the stress of practice (controllable).

The coach must never forget that the stress of daily routines (uncontrollable by the coach) will be added to the stress of practice (controllable).

As the athlete moves from the preparatory phase to the competition phase, the emphasis changes dramatically. There will be significant changes in the percentage of the cycle devoted to the specific areas, for example:

1.	Strength training	25%	5 hours
2.	General conditioning	10%	2 hours
3.	Throwing	30%	6 hours
4.	Drills	20%	4 hours
5.	Plyometrics	9%	1.8 hours
6.	Medicine ball	6%	1.2 hours

In the foregoing example, the most apparent shift involved the time allotted to general conditioning (five-percent reduction) and the three-percent increase in throwing volume. As we move from the preparatory phase, the majority of the conditioning has been achieved, and at this point, the conditioning emphasis is merely to maintain a fitness level sufficient to execute the volume of throws and other activities necessary for success. Not surprisingly, the volume of throwing will increase during this period, as we strive for success in the ring. As before, these percentages will shift as the athlete progresses through the competitive season to the point where the percentages of time devoted to some areas (e.g., plyometrics) fall to zero. Also, remember that these numbers serve to merely illustrate one possible scenario: it is the coach and the athlete who decide the specifics.

For a mono-cycle, assuming a 13-week competitive phase, a collegiate athlete would have a 30-week preparatory phase. In terms of strength training, the initial portion of this period will be spent on anatomical adaptation, followed by a maximum-strength segment, a conversion to power, and then a maintenance period, for example:

•	September 27-November 3	Anatomical adaptation
•	November 6-February 4	Maximum strength
	• Hypertrophy phase	
	• Strength phase	
	• Hypertrophy phase II	
	• Strength phase II	
•	February 7-April 1	Conversion to power
•	April 4-June 30	Maintenance

With a typical collegiate academic schedule, unloading periods often evolve naturally.

The aforementioned example illustrates a possible breakdown of the various phases of the strength-training program. With a typical collegiate academic schedule, unloading periods often evolve naturally. If this scenario is not the case, then the coach will need to insert unloading into the workouts. A similar calendar can be followed for the post-collegiate athlete with the necessary temporal adjustments. The training may begin a bit earlier, and the peak should occur later at the USATF Championships or in international competition.

The Bi-Cycle

Compared with the mono-cycle, the bi-cycle addresses similar early considerations, but involves a briefer period of anatomical adaptation and an earlier emphasis on strength and power. In addition to the 13-week spring competitive phase, there will also be an 11-to-12 week indoor competitive period to consider, for example:

•	September 27-October 21	Anatomical adaptation
•	October 24-January 27	Maximum strength
	◦ Hypertrophy phase	
	◦ Strength phase	
	◦ Hypertrophy phase II	
	◦ Strength phase II	
•	January 30-February 17	Conversion to power
•	February 20-Marcy 10	Maintenance
•	March 13-April 21	Maximum strength II
•	April 24-May 19	Conversion to power II
•	May 22-June 30	Maintenance

The aforementioned schedule illustrates a possible strength-program template for a bi-cycle. Ancillary exercises, such as running, medicine ball, and plyometrics, should follow a similar outline. For example, short sprints and depth jumps should occur during the conversion to the power phase. Likewise, medicine ball routines should be of shorter duration and higher intensity as the athlete endeavors to peak.

Following the completion of the indoor competitive season, the athlete returns to higher-volume workouts for a short period of time. The latter portion of a bi-cycle should resemble the corresponding portions of the mono-cycle program, because the goal remains the same—outstanding hammer performance at the appropriate meet.

Summary

Regardless of whether the athlete is undertaking a mono-cycle or a bi-cycle, the coach must establish the time parameters involved. While, in most instances, the mono-cycle is set up upon a ten-to-11 month calendar, there are exceptions. For instance, the 2006 Commonwealth Games were held in Melbourne, Australia. As a result, a greatly condensed cycle necessitated that a determination be made concerning what exercises should be utilized. This decision included not only the lifts to be executed during specific phases of training, but also the drills, plyometric exercises, medicine ball routines, and even the amount of time devoted to a specific weight implement. Once those factors had been ascertained, the coach could set up the plan and establish daily workouts.

It cannot be over-emphasized that daily evaluations of the athletes' status have to occur to determine the actual specifics of any workout. Once both what the athletes

Regardless of whether the athlete is undertaking a mono-cycle or a bi-cycle, the coach must establish the time parameters involved.

need and what they can execute have been identified, and then practice can begin. The evaluation does not end there though. Even during practice, the coach must watch for indications that the workout may need to be altered. These cues may be technical in nature or based upon results. If an athlete appears technically sound, yet the results are less than desired, it may be necessary to modify or end practice.

No secret formula to success exists. Rather, there are several fundamentals that must be observed, and within this framework, there exists the flexibility for the coach and athlete to attain the balance that leads to personal best performance. The fundamentals to be considered included developing the capacity of the athlete to get into and out of proper positions and the overall general fitness that enables the individual to work at a high level. This philosophy has helped in the development of athletes who finished sixth in the 25-pound weight at the 2005 USATF indoor championships, and who earned the bronze medal in the Central American-Caribbean championships.

Harvard has employed the following medicine ball and plyometric routines over the past decade. It is important to note that these workouts are not a panacea. Rather, these routines can serve as a menu for the coach to choose from each year. Keep in mind that not all routines will be utilized each year, nor will all athletes perform the same routine. As previously noted, determining an individual's strengths and needs should serve as the basis for what routine that athlete should perform.

> **Even during practice, the coach must watch for indications that the workout may need to be altered.**

Alex Livesey/Getty Images Sport

No secret formula to success exists.

Medicine Ball Workouts

Workout A

- 2 x 8 chest passes (extend and flip)
- 2 x 8 forward overheads
- 2 x 8 backward overheads
- 2 x 8 forward between the legs (emphasize the legs)
- 2 x 8 side passes (each side)
- 2 x 8 hammer throws (each side)

Workout B

- 2 x 10 chest passes (extend and flip)
- 2 x 10 forward overheads
- 2 x 10 backward overheads
- 2 x 10 forward between the legs (emphasize the legs)
- 2 x 10 side passes (each side)
- 2 x 10 hammer throws (each side)

Workout C

- 3 x 8 chest passes (extend and flip)
- 3 x 8 forward overheads
- 3 x 8 backward overheads
- 3 x 8 forward between the legs (emphasize the legs)
- 3 x 8 side passes (each side)
- 3 x 8 hammer throws (each side)

Workout D

- 3 x 10 chest passes (extend and flip)
- 3 x 10 forward overheads
- 3 x 10 backward overheads
- 3 x 10 forward between the legs (emphasize the legs)
- 3 x 10 side passes (each side)
- 3 x 10 hammer throws (each side)

Workout E

- 3 x 15 quick wall bounces
- 3 x 15 trunk rotations
- 3 x 15 bench flips

Plyometric Workouts

Workout A

- 2 x 10 squat jumps
- 2 x 10 split-squat jumps
- 2 x 10 cycled split-squat jumps
- 2 x 10 medicine ball sit-ups
- 2 x 10 plyometric sit-ups

Workout B

- 2 x 10 split-squat jumps
- 2 x 10 cycled split-squat jumps
- 2 x 10 double-leg hops
- 2 x 10 bound
- 2 x 10 medicine ball sit-ups
- 2 x 10 plyometric sit-ups

Workout C

- 3 x 10 double-leg tuck jumps
- 3 x 10 pike jump
- 3 x 10 double-leg hops
- 3 x 10 hop-bounds
- 2 x 10 medicine ball sit-ups
- 2 x 10 plyometric sit-ups

Workout D

- 3 x 10 double-leg hops
- 3 x 10 hop-bounds
- 3 x 10 double-leg speed hops
- 3 x 10 single-leg hops (each leg)
- 2 x 10 medicine ball sit-ups
- 2 x 10 plyometric sit-ups

Workout E

- 3 x 10 single-leg hops (each leg)
- 3 x 10 hop-bounds
- 3 x 10 double-leg ons
- 3 x 10 double-leg overs
- 2 x 10 medicine ball sit-ups
- 2 x 10 plyometric sit-ups

Workout F

- 3 x 10 double-leg ons
- 3 x 10 double leg-overs
- 3 x 10 double-leg on-overs
- 3 x 10 bound

Workout G

- 4 x 10 double-leg ons
- 4 x 10 double-leg overs
- 4 x 10 double-leg on-overs

Workout H

- 5 x 8 depth jumps

Workout I

- 3 x 10 velocity builder

Workout J

- 3 x 12 velocity builder

Workout K

- 4 x 10 velocity builder

Workout L

- 4 x 12 velocity builder

Workout M

- 3 x 15 velocity builder

Workout N

- 4 x 15 velocity builder

Plyometrics Circuit

- First   110M hurdle mark: 10 x squat jumps
           Return to start

- Second   110M hurdle mark: 10 x split-squat jumps
           Return to start

- Third   110M hurdle mark: 10 x cycled split-squat jumps
           Return to start

- Fourth   110M hurdle mark: 10 x double-leg tuck jumps
           Return to start

- Fifth   110M hurdle mark: 10 x pike jumps
           Return to start

- Sixth   110M hurdle mark: 10 x sit-ups
           Return to start

- Seventh   110M hurdle mark: 10 x plyometric push-up
           Return to start

* Special thanks to coach Shawn Schleizer, CSCS for his editing help on this article.

33

Strategic Thinking in Throws Practice: Applying Concepts from Industrial/Organizational Psychology and the Business World to the Track and Field Environment

By Paul E. Turner, Ph.D.

> **Successful coaching is dependent upon the interaction of physiology, biomechanics, and psychology.**

Coaches rightfully view training plans in terms of microcycles, mesocycles, and macrocycles in establishing work loads, yet should look beyond merely physiological factors when establishing the annual training plan. Successful coaching is dependent upon the interaction of physiology, biomechanics, and psychology. While the biomechanical aspect generally focuses on technical improvements, the work volume involved in this aspect should also be considered as the training plan is developed.

The basic focus of this article is to emphasize the fact that coaches must explore what other fields have to offer them, in this case, the areas of industrial/organizational psychology and business. Examining other philosophies and points of view makes it easier to put training and planning in the proper perspective.

Prior to the initiation of a strategic plan, the coach should become familiar with the components of strategic thinking and the formation and implementation involved in those components. As the following chart illustrates, strategic thinking is cyclical in nature and is a continuous process.

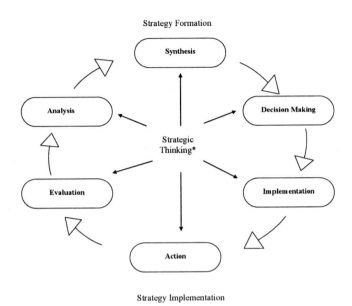

Strategy Formation

Synthesis

Decision Making

Analysis

Strategic Thinking*

Implementation

Evaluation

Action

Strategy Implementation

* Used with permission from *Strategic Thinking and Decision Making*, Harvard University Center for Workplace Development

Strategic Planning

Despite what may seem to be the obvious efficacy of strategic planning, it is of value to express the purposes of such planning. In any given scenario a variety of purposes exist. In terms of the realm of throwing and the training associated with throwing, the following steps have been identified as being pertinent:

- Identify the aspirations and challenges
- Clarify and gain consensus around the strategy
- Identify and align strategic initiatives
- Measure and evaluate progress in achieving vision and strategy
- Direct skill building efforts
- Guide resource allocation

Similar to the various training cycles, the following four levels of planning should be considered as a training program is developed:

- Tactical
- Operational
- Interactive
- Strategic

Each of the levels involves unique desired results, style of action, and underlying value. The Center for Workplace Development (CWD) at Harvard has developed a matrix for these planning levels. For the tactical-planning level, the desired result is to satisfy customer expectations and to solve problems, while the operational level involves maintaining the status quo, conforming to expectations, controlling results, and turning plans into action. The next highest planning level, interactive, is concerned with anticipating daily problems and exceeding expectations. The strategic-planning level is concerned with achieving the ideal future and optimizing outcomes, given resources and constraints.

The style of action particular to the tactical-planning level is reactive in nature. For the operational-planning level the style of action has a short-term focus, fixes problems, and is concerned with maintaining a smooth operation. The interactive level is proactive in nature, and the strategic-planning level is future-minded, has a long-term focus, and is very much a route to explore alternative possibilities. The underlying value of the tactical plan is survival and responsiveness. For the operational level the focus is stability and control. The two highest planning levels (interactive and strategic) are concerned with continuous improvement (interactive) and controlled instability and optimization of opportunities (strategic). Most coaches operate the majority of the time in the interactive- and operational-planning levels. While this can lead to success, it also limits the potential long-term growth and development of the athlete.

Most coaches operate the majority of the time in the interactive- and operational-planning levels.

According to the CWD, strategic thinking involves five components:

- Having a clear vision of the ideal future.
- Drawing on and being shaped by the organization's core values.
- Continuously scanning the environment for opportunities and threats.
- Attending to the patterns and relationships and circumstances.
- Recognizing the interconnections and interdependencies before making decisions.

Strategic Planning Stages

Strategic planning moves through four stages. The first stage is conducting a SWOT analysis. SWOT represents **S**trengths, **W**eaknesses, **O**pportunities, and **T**hreats. The coach should conduct this analysis prior to developing a training program. This endeavor involves gathering performance data (e.g., lifting information, distances, etc.), identifying statutes and laws that affect the organization (NCAA rules regarding practice, number of competitions, eligibility, etc.), defining the current mission and goals, assessing how successful the organization has been in the past in achieving goals (was the athlete successful in the past), gather data from stakeholders on their perception of the organization (input from athletes and coaches), and determining the external forces influencing the organization's future (access to facilities, travel budget, equipment budget, etc.). When addressing the effort to develop a training plan for an individual, the coach must specifically identify the following factors:

☐ Strengths: what does the individual do well.

☐ Weaknesses: from a technical as well as strength perspective. Also evaluate other components of the training model.

☐ Opportunities for the individual: meet schedule and practice calendar are important aspects of this part of the first stage of strategic thinking.

☐ Threats to the individual: overtraining, staleness, injury potential, conflicts with facilities, academic conflicts, etc.

The second stage of strategic planning is creating a shared vision. This step is accomplished by involving others in the planning process and attending to stated policies. For example, the Harvard Department of Athletics defines their mission as providing athletics for all students, with opportunities for practice and competition appropriate to their interest and skills. Further, Harvard defines success in athletics, based upon performance within the Ivy League. By definition, each coach at Harvard shares this vision, but of course, success at the national level would also result in success at the Ivy League level, so the two are not mutually exclusive. The involvement of other coaches and the athletes enhances the likelihood of developing a shared vision. Determine the expectations and aspirations of your charges and assimilate them into your plan. The athletes often have insights that we cannot possess unless they share them with us.

The third stage of strategic planning is the identification of critical issues and the development of specific goals and plans. At this stage the strengths, weaknesses, opportunities, and threats are identified, and each area is clarified for action. As this step is completed, a detailed action plan defining goals/outcomes, performance/success measures, actions to be taken, personnel involved in the prescribed actions, and the timeline of the plan is developed. Throwing lends itself very readily to the application stage in that it is so quantifiable. Distances achieved, weights lifted, and place at the conference meet or nationals all are measures of performance that are very functional and objective.

The final stage of strategic planning involves developing the operational plan. As the plan is developed, it is monitored, evaluated, and revised. One of the most important actions to be taken at this stage is the initiation of collaborative efforts to achieve synergy and to avoid duplication. For example, if plyometrics are part of your training plan, it is important to communicate with the strength and conditioning staff to insure that they are not also prescribing plyometric workouts (or at least are doing them in conjunction with your plan in order to avoid potentially dangerous overloads). This action also reduces the risk of the silo effect (when an individual becomes so isolated in terms of planning that he is totally reliant upon himself). Likewise, an active role by the strength and conditioning personnel in the development of the strategic plan encourages strategic thinking (and also results in the throwers attaining a status approaching that of football players in the weight room). Regular checks on progress occur during this stage of planning. Results should be assessed against critical success factors and individual goal measures. This evaluation could involve testing in the weightroom, occasional implementation of Quadathlon tests, and, as a minimum, subjective attention to distances achieved in practice.

The athletes often have insights that coaches cannot possess unless they share them with their coaches.

Biases in Decision Making that Could Influence the Training Plan

There are many possible biases that can influence a coach's thinking and decision-making abilities.

There are many possible biases that can influence a coach's thinking and decision-making abilities. The coach must be aware of these factors in order to enhance the chance of producing the best possible plan. As coaches plan, they should be introspective. In that regard, the following list* of possible biases can help facilitate the process as coaches weigh their decisions against the biases:

☐ Search for supportive evidence: Gathering support for a particular perspective while disregarding information that threatens a view.

☐ Inconsistency: Not applying the same decision criteria in similar situations.

☐ Conservatism: Reluctance or failure to change perspective when presented new information.

☐ Recency: The most recent events or information overshadow those from the past.

☐ Availability: Relying upon specific events easily recalled from memory while excluding other information.

☐ Anchoring: Essentially the opposite of recency. Decisions are unduly influenced by initial information. Also known as the primacy effect.

☐ Illusory correlations: Accepting causal relationships when none exist.

☐ Selective perception: Basing decisions upon your own background and experience.

☐ Attribution of success and failure: Success is because of the planner, and failure is because of someone else.

☐ Optimism-wishful thinking: Preference for future outcomes affects forecasts of such outcomes.

☐ Underestimating uncertainty: Being overly optimistic, making unjustified correlations, and the need to reduce anxiety causes the individual to underestimate uncertainty. "If s/he follows the plan, success is guaranteed."

* From Harvard's Center for Workplace Development

Putting it All Together

A SWOT analysis is conducted for each thrower prior to initiation of the training plan. The following example illustrates an analysis for a shot putter:

☐ Strengths: Thrower moves well from the back of the ring to the middle; has good balance, rhythm, and good position in the middle. Good upper-body strength.

☐ Weaknesses: Poor shift from middle to front. Drops elbow. Lower-body strength not good. Explosiveness is lacking.

☐ Opportunities: Practice, competitions, weightroom access.

☐ Threats: Injuries, NCAA regulations, academic demands, teen angst, logistical conflicts (e.g., the track is closed for renovation).

Once this analysis is conducted, the coach begins the process off creating a shared vision with all individuals involved in the strategic plan. The coach should sit down and encourage the athlete to contribute his ideas. Listen to what each thrower thinks that he needs in terms of training. Bring the strength coaches on board to discuss their ideas and to integrate the plans (and to make sure that they are producing a lifting program that is not only effective, but also congruent with the throwing and competition schedules, for example, one that results in peak strength and power levels in April may not serve anyone). These interactions reduce the possibility of resistance to the plan occurring, by the athlete or by other professionals within the organization.

As the planning process moves into the third stage, the emphasis shifts to prioritizing the issues from those having greatest-to-least impact on the vision. The key issue that the plan must address is how the training plan can best utilize the time and resources available to result in the highest performance levels. It is at this stage that a detailed action plan spelling out goals, measures of performance, actions to be taken, personnel involvement, and the timeline begin to emerge. The roles of individuals in the process are defined, from strength and conditioning staff to sports medicine and nutritionists. The team utilized in the training regimen begins to emerge.

The fourth stage begins taking shape, as the reporting and communication networks are identified to facilitate accountability. Everyone needs to be on the same page. Measurement and progress reports are built into the processes of each area of the team. Reports from strength staff, in terms of lifting progress, sports medicine information, etc., all need to be considered in the strategic perspective. As information becomes available to the coach, including practice and meet performances, adjustments to the plan are made, if necessary. Training plans are written in ink, not carved in stone. All variables need to be considered on a daily basis and within the macrocycle. It is also during this stage that attention needs to be paid to resource allocation. One of the greatest limitations to the college track coach is the 20-hour-per-week restriction. The strategic plan must consider how these precious hours are utilized. Does the plan involve 10 hours of lifting, five hours of throwing, and five hours of activities such as medicine ball and plyometrics or is there a greater emphasis on throwing volume and technical training? During which phase of the macrocycle do these proportions shift?

Having identified issues during the SWOT analysis, the coach then has to address how to rectify these issues. Areas that have been identified as strengths require less attention, but must not be ignored lest they become weaknesses. The previous examples of weaknesses can be attacked with drills and standing throws for the technical issues, while the lower-body strength deficit can be rectified with proper weightlifting work. Activities such as plyometrics, medicine ball routines, and sprinting can help with the explosiveness issue. Opportunities occur each day during practice and with competitions. Threats such as injury can be reduced by proper coaching, while, unfortunately, some issues are beyond the control of the coach. Attention to events that are beyond the control of the coach should be minimized in that this factor could result in a drain on limited resources. Because any number of ways to address

Having identified issues during the SWOT analysis, the coach then has to address how to rectify these issues.

specific issues exists, no single correct answer to these issues is available. The following example illustrates a potential microcycle training period that would address the issues uncovered with the SWOT:

Monday	Tuesday	Wednesday	Thursday	Friday
25 Stands	25 Stands	15 Stands	15 Stands	10 Stands
Drills	Drills	Drills	Drills	Drills
5 X 30 Sprint	Med Ball	10 Fulls	10 Fulls	15 Fulls
Weights		Sprints	Plyometrics	Med Ball
Emphasis on legs		Weights		Weights
		Emphasis on legs		Emphasis on legs

The time breakdown for this week may be 4.5 hours lifting, .5 hours sprinting, 6.25 hours throwing, 2.5 hours of drills, 1 of hour medicine ball, and 1 hour plyometrics (15.75 of the NCAA allowable 20 hours). Add two hours of film analysis and the week totals 17.75 hours. This time allocation will shift throughout the year. For example, during competition, three hours additional per week or so are incorporated into an individual's schedule, necessitating a reduction in some area because of the practice restrictions. Likewise, the specific points of emphasis during the year will change, and plans need to be flexible to accommodate such changes.

The specific points of training emphasis during the year will change, and plans need to be flexible to accommodate such changes.

Matthew Stockman/Getty Images Sport

Coaches should make every attempt to be objective and systematic in developing each athlete's training program.

Conclusions

To be successful, coaches must look to the future as they develop their training plans. Have a vision and continue to grow as coaches so that the athletes that you work with can continue to grow. Avoid biases in the decision-making process. Examine other perspectives and be flexible throughout the entire training cycle. Every attempt should be made to be objective and systematic in developing each individual's training program. Be willing to take from other academic and professional areas and apply whatever you glean from them to your plans. Strategic thinking and decision making can enhance the experience for both the coach and the athlete.

To be successful, coaches must look to the future as they develop their training plans.

34

Critical Factors in the Shot Put

By Mike Young

Operational Terminology

Flight phase: The duration of time where the athlete is moving towards the front of the throwing circle and has no contact with the throwing surface. In the glide technique, this is the period of time beginning when the rear foot breaks contact with the throwing surface until it makes contact again with the throwing surface. In the spin technique, this is the period of time beginning when the front foot leaves the throwing surface until the rear foot makes contact with the throwing surface.

Power position: The position that is achieved when the front foot touches down, and the athlete has both feet in contact with the throwing surface in preparation for the delivery of the throw.

Rear foot: The foot that is towards the rear of the throwing circle when the athlete is in the power position.

Front foot: The foot that is closest to the toe board when the athlete is in the power position.

Rear foot touchdown: The point at which the thrower's rear foot makes contact with the throwing circle, following the flight phase.

Front foot touchdown: The point at which the thrower's front foot makes contact with the throwing circle, following the flight phase.

Transition phase: Following the flight phase, this is the period of time between rear- and front-foot contact with the throwing circle.

Shoulder-hip separation: The orientation of the hips, relative to the orientation of the shoulders. A neutral position, or zero degrees of separation, occurs when the shoulders and hips are aligned with one another, as would be the case in anatomical position. A positive angle occurs when the throwing-side shoulder is posterior to the throwing-side hip.

Release: The first instant of non-contact between the shot and the thrower's hand.

Release velocity: The magnitude of the shot velocity at the moment of release.

Release angle: The angle at which the shot is released relative to horizontal.

Release height: The height of the center of the shot above the surface of the ring at the moment of release.

Horizontal release distance: The horizontal distance between the center of the shot and the innermost edge of the toe board at the moment of release.

Projected distance: The horizontal displacement of the shot, beginning at the point of horizontal release distance and ending at the landing point of the shot.

Measured distance: The horizontal displacement of the shot measured from the innermost edge of the toe board and ending at the landing point of the shot. This is the distance recorded as the official result. More specifically, the measured distance is the sum of the projected distance and the horizontal release distance.

Introduction

Considerable research has been performed on the shot put. Typically, these studies examined release velocity, release angle, and release height. Unfortunately, these three parameters paint an unclear picture. They indicate what needs to happen, but not what it takes to make it happen. Likewise, many coaching articles have been written which provide the author's concept of ideal technique. All of the information provided in these articles may not always be valid and correct. Some of the suggestions may be based on ideas passed down to the author, or on successes of former champions (who may have succeeded in spite of their technique), in addition to the personal ideas and biases of the coach. While often very useful, these methods of determination can create the possibility of faulty conclusions being drawn. The primary purpose of this article is to mesh together the scientific research with the suggestions and recommendations of coaches to present the critical factors for achieving elite-level success in the shot put.

The findings presented in this article are part of the ongoing research of the USOC & USATF's collaborative High Performance Plan (HPP) for the shot put. This project examines various parameters of the throw in hopes of uncovering the factors most critical to success. In the most simplistic sense, the critical factors are aspects of technique, which best predict elite-level performance. This information is passed on to elite athletes and their coaches to assist these athletes in their development and help them reach the medal stand in World Championships and Olympic Games. The goal is to provide helpful information to athletes and coaches in hopes of directing their technical development, identifying major flaws, and reinforcing strengths. The information is intended to be specific enough to be useful but general enough to account for the unique technical differences inherent in each athlete due to that individual's unique anthropometric, physiological, and stylistic characteristics. It should be noted, however, that the critical factors for elite athletes might not be the same for developmental throwers.

There are three main areas where data and information was collected to determine the critical factors. The first of these was a meta-analysis of previous biomechanical research on the shot put. A database of over 300 throws was created, with information compiled concerning shot puts from both genders at both elite and non-elite levels. In addition to this undertaking, an extensive review of previous coaching literature on the shot put and general throwing technique was examined and put through a "scientific filter" to weed out recommendations and suggestions, which had no foundation in the basic physics principles that govern human movement. In addition to this step, ongoing dialogue with current coaches and athletes has generated ideas for further investigation. Finally, and perhaps most importantly, ongoing research on today's top American throwers, incorporating the above two sources, is used to determine and verify the recommendations and uncover other critical factors that may not have been previously considered.

> **The projected distance of an object is determined largely by release height, release angle, and release velocity.**

As was previously stated, the goal of this project is to determine the underlying factors that contribute to the measured distance of an elite throw. The measured distance of a shot put throw can be broken down into two components (Figure 1). The first of these is the projected distance. This measure refers to the total distance through which the shot has displaced after leaving the hand of the thrower. The projected distance of the throw is determined by the release height, the angle of release, and the velocity of the shot at the point of release. These three parameters can be used to calculate the distance a projectile will travel using the projectile-motion equation (Figure 2). The second component that contributes to the measured distance is the release position, relative to the point of measurement, in this case, the toe-board. Of these two components, projected distance makes up to 97% of the measured distance.

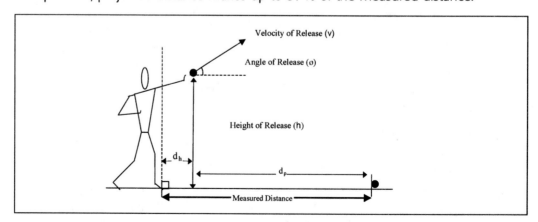

Figure 1. The measured distance of the throw is equal to the sum of the horizontal release distance relative to the toe board (dh) and the projected distance (dp).

Since projected distance is the overwhelming factor that contributes to the measured distance, it should be clear that it is important to have an understanding of the parameters that determine it. The projected distance of an object is determined largely by release height, release angle, and release velocity. In the case of the shot put, wind resistance and aerodynamic factors can be ignored. The equation that governs projectile motion (Figure 2) provides some clues as to the relative importance of each parameter.

Release height is the least important factor in the projectile-motion equation which is quite convenient, since little can be done to change release height, because it is primarily determined by the athlete's anthropometric parameters and to a lesser degree by the release angle. Release angle is the second most important factor in the projectile-motion equation and is determined by the angle of the throwing arm, as well as the orientation of the trunk relative to the ground. The final parameter in the projectile-motion equation is velocity. Projected distance is a function of velocity squared. Consequently, velocity is far and away the most influential of the release parameters. Taking this factor into account, it would be easy and convenient to consider release velocity as the main critical factor and simply have coaches and athletes strive to release as fast as possible.

Such an approach, however, would be flawed logic for three reasons. First, other than some specific practice situations, most shot putters typically try to throw as hard and fast as possible already. Telling them to do what they're already trying to do would be unnecessary. Second, the correlation between release velocity and measured distance is so strong, it would be redundant to use release velocity as a critical factor. Finally, using velocity as the critical factor paints a confusing picture, because while it may be the primary predictor of measured distance, it is actually a result of many other factors that lead up to that point, and, as a result, it should be considered as a product of the prior actions, rather than as a means to an end itself. With this point in mind, it is important to examine all parts of the throw to determine which factors positively affect the total distance of the throw.

> Release height is the least important factor in the projectile-motion equation.

$$d_{projected} = \frac{v^2 \sin 2\theta}{2g} \left[1 + \left[\frac{2gh}{v^2 \sin^2 \theta} \right]^{1/2} \right]$$

$d_{projected}$ – projected distance
v – release velocity
θ – release angle
g – gravitational acceleration, approximately 9.81 m/s^2
h – release height

Figure 2. The projectile motion equation. The projected distance of a throw is a result of release velocity, release angle, and release height. Note that projected distance is a function of velocity squared.

The following list details the factors that have been determined to be critical to achieving elite level success in the shot put. For simplicity and organizational sake, the critical factors have been grouped into release, kinematic, and temporal categories. While thorough, this list is by no means completely comprehensive, and new critical factors may, in fact, be identified in the future as research continues. Also, the relative importance of each critical factor will vary for each athlete, depending on such aspects as gender, anthropometry, strength parameters, throwing technique used (glide or spin), and individual stylistic elements.

Release Parameters

As was previously noted, the release parameters are what actually determine the measured distance of the throw. In theory, the projectile-motion equation could easily be used to find optimal-release parameters that would result in a given distance. These mathematically determined optimal-release parameters could then be used as goals for training. Using this method, however, would be an effort in futility. The primary reason for such a conclusion is that in humans, the release parameters are not independent of one another as is assumed by the equation. This dependency phenomenon is due to the fact that unlike man-made projectile machines, like cannons and catapults, the human musculoskeletal system is an extremely complex system of levers and pulleys, which do not function with equal capacities at all angles or positions. Attempting to achieve mathematically optimal release parameters would most certainly result in shorter measured distances. It is with this factor in mind that we can establish "real world" critical factors for the release parameters.

Because of the significance of release velocity, all other release parameters should only be examined with regard to their affect on this most important parameter. While the dependence of the release parameters is a quite complex phenomenon, a basic understanding will suffice for the purpose of this article. It is sufficient to know that release velocity and release angle exhibit a strong inverse relationship. In other words, for any given thrower, as one of the parameters increases, the other decreases. Keeping this point in mind, it should be obvious that one of the simplest ways to increase the release velocity, and thus measured distance, is to manipulate the release angle so that it maximizes release velocity, while still maintaining an angle that will permit elite-level distances.

> Because of the significance of release velocity, all other release parameters should only be examined with regard to their affect on this most important parameter.

☐ Increased Release Velocity

Release velocity is undoubtedly the most important factor in determining the distance of a throw. Release velocities in excess of 13 m/s are necessary for elite-level throws. As such, all attempts should be made to maximize release velocity. This recommendation, however, must be made with the caution and advice that increasing either the athlete or the implement velocity at one phase of the throw will not necessarily increase velocity at release. In fact, HPP research has indicated that the opposite may be the case. This situation is most likely due to the fact that increasing velocity prematurely can result in instability, technical problems, decreased muscle loading, or inefficient sequencing of muscle contractions.

☐ Lower Release Angle

The primary importance of release angle is its effect on the release velocity. As long as the release angle is within a range permitting elite-level throws, it should be optimized to enable greater release velocities. In so doing, the measured distance will be greater. HPP research has indicated that for humans, the release parameters are optimized when the angle of release is between 31-and-36 degrees. This span is considerably lower than the mathematically "optimal" range of 40-to-43 degrees for elite throwers determined by using the projectile-motion equation. While it is impractical for coaches and athletes to aim for exact release angles, it is important to know that lower release angles are actually advantageous as long as they still permit elite-level throws, and that the mathematically optimal release angles will more than likely result in decreased throwing distances.

□ Greater Horizontal-Release Distance

HPP research has indicated that the horizontal-release position, relative to the toe board, is a critical factor to throwing success. The optimal horizontal-release position should be between 0.2m and 0.5m in front of the toe board, with this distance being largely determined by the anthropometry and technique of the athlete. This distance itself makes up only about two-to-three percent of the measured distance, but this does not reflect the potential benefits of a longer path of implement acceleration. With this point in mind, the horizontal-release position is significant for both its potential to create an advantageous (or disadvantageous) release point and also because it can be an indication of a greater range of force application to the implement.

When most coaches and athletes refer to "technique," they are primarily speaking of an athlete's kinematics.

Kinematic Parameters

Kinematic parameters are those factors that relate to the movements of the body without regard to the forces that cause those movements. When most coaches and athletes refer to "technique," they are primarily speaking of an athlete's kinematics. Six critical factors have been identified in this category:

□ Long Sweeping Free Leg (Rotational Technique)

A long sweeping free leg refers to the non-support leg on a rotational thrower, as they are making the turn and subsequent flight phase to enter the center of the circle. A wide sweep of the free leg will help to maximize the rotary momentum of the rotational thrower as they enter the flight phase and will assist in developing greater positive separation (Figure 3) between the shoulders and hips at rear-foot touchdown. The correct execution of the free leg should be characterized by a great toe-to-toe distance (Figure 4), a wide radius about the free leg-hip axis, and a sweep that is low enough to the throwing surface to not disturb balance, but high enough to optimize the effective radius of the leg.

Figure 3: Shoulder-hip orientations for right-handed thrower. The dashed line represents the orientation of

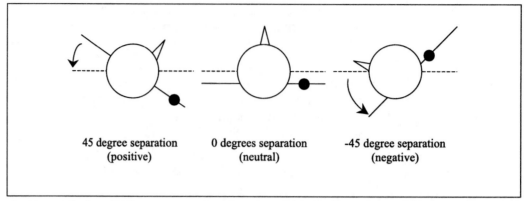

the hips, while the solid line represents the orientation of the shoulders. The small black circle represents the shot. The angle between the line of the shoulder and the line of the hip represents the shoulder-hip orientation. Athletes should attempt to maximize positive separation at rear-foot touchdown. At release, negative shoulder-hip orientations should be avoided in favor of a neutral orientation.

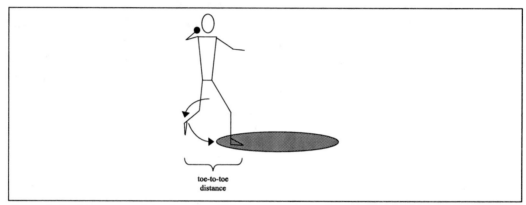

Figure 4: A wide sweep of the free leg will help to maximize the rotary momentum of the rotational thrower, as his rear foot touches down near the center of the ring and will assist in developing greater positive separation between the shoulders and hips during the power position.

☐ Higher Center of Mass during Flight Phase (Glide Technique)

It has previously been thought that the path of both the athlete's center of mass and the shot should ideally travel in a linear path, with the lowest point being at the beginning of the throw and the highest point being at the moment of release. Recent research, however, has shown that this may not be the case. In fact, HPP research has indicated that the S-shaped path (Figure 5) of both the thrower's center of mass and the shot, as seen in the sagittal plane of most throws, is not something to be corrected but is actually advantageous. This undulation creates an opportunity to activate the stretch reflex upon landing and in so doing increases the muscle activation of the legs.

The stretch reflex is an involuntary reflex contraction of a muscle in response to the stretching of an attached tendon or the muscle itself. When the rate of length change in a muscle is great, this involuntary reflex creates more forceful and powerful muscular contractions than would be possible under voluntary control alone. The response of the muscles to the reflex is directly related to the rate of the stretch. As such, an increased rate of stretch will result in increased involuntary muscle activation via the stretch reflex.

In the shot put, the rate of stretch can be enhanced by maximizing the vertical velocity of the athlete when he lands following the flight phase. This objective can be achieved by increasing the maximal height of the athlete's center of mass during this period. The higher the apex of the center of mass during the flight phase, the greater the athlete's vertical velocity should be upon landing. Every athlete will have an optimal height that will primarily be determined by their eccentric strength and the capacity of their nervous system to respond to sudden changes in muscle length. The important point though is that an increased center of mass height achieved during the flight phase is not an error and can, in fact, be advantageous.

☐ Greater Rear-Knee Flexion at Rear Foot-Touchdown

HPP research has indicated that greater rear-knee flexion at rear-foot touchdown is one of the best indicators of success in the shot put. The ideal rear-knee angle at rear-foot touchdown should be approximately 100 degrees, with this value being highly dependent on the strength of the athlete. Most athletes land in a position with much greater extension of the rear-knee joint. Greater flexion of the rear knee at rear-foot touchdown may provide an opportunity for the musculature of the rear leg to function with favorable leverage and operate through the strongest portion of its force curve. This scenario would result in greater implement acceleration. Greater rear-knee flexion may also be indicative of the position of the athlete's center of mass relative to their base of support as well as the position of the shot relative to the hip. Both of these points have been suggested by coaches as important factors for the shot put. It must be noted; however, that knee flexion beyond the proposed optimal value could potentially have a greater negative effect on the throw than having lesser flexion. The depth of knee flexion, which results in decreased performance, has yet to be determined.

Greater rear-knee flexion at rear-foot touchdown is one of the best indicators of success in the shot put.

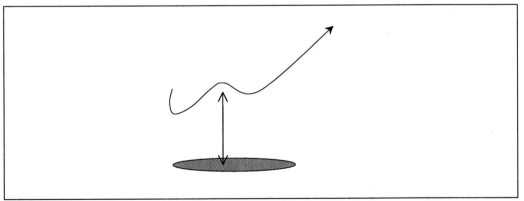

Figure 5: Undulation of shot path, as seen in the sagittal view of a thrower using the glide technique. A higher apex of the initial peak should result in a greater activation of the leg musculature upon landing.

☐ Greater Shoulder-Hip Separation at Rear-Foot Touchdown

Positive shoulder-hip separation as defined by this article has long been advocated by throws coaches (Figure 3). HPP research has provided evidence that a greater degree of separation is advantageous to maximize throwing distance. This situation is most likely due to the fact that greater separation between the shoulders and hips at rear-foot touchdown creates more pre-tension in the abdominal musculature and also creates a longer path around which the shot can travel before being released. This factor provides the opportunity to increase the time of force application to the implement and, in so doing, accelerate the shot to a greater extent.

☐ Greater Rear-Knee Flexion at Release

HPP research has indicated that greater rear-knee flexion at release is a significant predictor of the measured distance. This conclusion is in stark contrast to the recommendation that complete or near-complete extension of the rear or both legs is crucial for achieving maximum distance. The reason for this discrepancy may lie in the fact that the rear-knee angle at release may not be a critical factor in and of itself, but rather an indication or effect of the extreme power and explosiveness needed to be an elite-level shot putter. A similar phenomenon has been seen in sprinting, jumping for height, and Olympic weightlifting. In such a case, the initial force generated by the legs accelerates the athlete and shot system with such rapidity that the shot is either released prior to the point of complete extension of the legs or the athlete breaks contact with the ground, making further extension of the legs inconsequential. As such, it may very well be advisable to instruct athletes to strive for complete extension of one or both legs, but those athletes who are very explosive may never have the opportunity to even approach full extension.

☐ Neutral Shoulder-Hip Orientation at Release

The results of HPP research have indicated that a neutral shoulder-hip orientation at release will help to maximize throwing distance (Figure 3). This finding is most likely because small or nonexistent shoulder-hip separation is an indication of a strong non-throwing side block. Such a block would result in a transfer of momentum from the non-throwing side to the throwing side, which would, in turn, increase the velocity of the throwing side and implement.

A neutral shoulder-hip orientation at release will help to maximize throwing distance.

Temporal Parameters

Temporal parameters are often mentioned in coaching literature, but there is little evidence to suggest that the many timing patterns previously suggested have any significant effect on the outcome of the throw. In fact, only one temporal parameter appeared to have any effect at all on the distance achieved—a short transition time.

☐ Short Transition Time (Glide Technique)

The transition time is the period of time following flight phase between rear- and front-foot touchdown. A short transition time appears to be beneficial for throwers using the glide technique, but no such benefit has been seen in rotational throwers. A near simultaneous rear- and front-foot touchdown may either allow for force application from both legs sooner in the throw or permit the athlete to vault himself over an extended front leg, depending on the technique of the athlete. Both of these methods have been suggested by coaches as effective techniques for throwing the shot.

Conclusions

The conclusions of this project are significant, because they validate some of the previous theories on shot putting and refute those that were not valid. Given the results, it is important to note that they do not apply equally to all throwers. Likewise, they are most likely not the most critical factors to the success of a novice or sub-elite thrower. These critical factors do, however, provide valuable information for coaches and elite shot putters and should be used as a guideline for technical development.

Andy Lyons/Getty Images Sport